Modern Critical Interpretations

D. H. Lawrence's
The Rainbow

Modern Critical Interpretations

The Oresteia
Beowulf
The General Prologue to
  The Canterbury Tales
The Pardoner's Tale
The Knight's Tale
The Divine Comedy
Exodus
Genesis
The Gospels
The Iliad
The Book of Job
Volpone
Doctor Faustus
The Revelation of St.
  John the Divine
The Song of Songs
Oedipus Rex
The Aeneid
The Duchess of Malfi
Antony and Cleopatra
As You Like It
Coriolanus
Hamlet
Henry IV, Part I
Henry IV, Part II
Henry V
Julius Caesar
King Lear
Macbeth
Measure for Measure
The Merchant of Venice
A Midsummer Night's
  Dream
Much Ado About
  Nothing
Othello
Richard II
Richard III
The Sonnets
Taming of the Shrew
The Tempest
Twelfth Night
The Winter's Tale
Emma
Mansfield Park
Pride and Prejudice
The Life of Samuel
  Johnson
Moll Flanders
Robinson Crusoe
Tom Jones
The Beggar's Opera
Gray's Elegy
Paradise Lost
The Rape of the Lock
Tristram Shandy
Gulliver's Travels

Evelina
The Marriage of Heaven
  and Hell
Songs of Innocence and
  Experience
Jane Eyre
Wuthering Heights
Don Juan
The Rime of the Ancient
  Mariner
Bleak House
David Copperfield
Hard Times
A Tale of Two Cities
Middlemarch
The Mill on the Floss
Jude the Obscure
The Mayor of
  Casterbridge
The Return of the Native
Tess of the D'Urbervilles
The Odes of Keats
Frankenstein
Vanity Fair
Barchester Towers
The Prelude
The Red Badge of
  Courage
The Scarlet Letter
The Ambassadors
Daisy Miller, The Turn
  of the Screw, and
  Other Tales
The Portrait of a Lady
Billy Budd, Benito Cer-
  eno, Bartleby the Scriv-
  ener, and Other Tales
Moby-Dick
The Tales of Poe
Walden
Adventures of
  Huckleberry Finn
The Life of Frederick
  Douglass
Heart of Darkness
Lord Jim
Nostromo
A Passage to India
Dubliners
A Portrait of the Artist as
  a Young Man
Ulysses
Kim
The Rainbow
Sons and Lovers
Women in Love
1984
Major Barbara

Man and Superman
Pygmalion
St. Joan
The Playboy of the
  Western World
The Importance of Being
  Earnest
Mrs. Dalloway
To the Lighthouse
My Antonia
An American Tragedy
Murder in the Cathedral
The Waste Land
Absalom, Absalom!
Light in August
Sanctuary
The Sound and the Fury
The Great Gatsby
A Farewell to Arms
The Sun Also Rises
Arrowsmith
Lolita
The Iceman Cometh
Long Day's Journey Into
  Night
The Grapes of Wrath
Miss Lonelyhearts
The Glass Menagerie
A Streetcar Named
  Desire
Their Eyes Were
  Watching God
Native Son
Waiting for Godot
Herzog
All My Sons
Death of a Salesman
Gravity's Rainbow
All the King's Men
The Left Hand of
  Darkness
The Brothers Karamazov
Crime and Punishment
Madame Bovary
The Interpretation of
  Dreams
The Castle
The Metamorphosis
The Trial
Man's Fate
The Magic Mountain
Montaigne's Essays
Remembrance of Things
  Past
The Red and the Black
Anna Karenina
War and Peace

These and other titles in preparation

D. H. Lawrence's
The Rainbow

Edited and with an introduction by

Harold Bloom
Sterling Professor of the Humanities
Yale University

Chelsea House Publishers ◊ *1988*
NEW YORK ◊ NEW HAVEN ◊ PHILADELPHIA

Library of Congress Cataloging-in-Publication Data
D. H. Lawrence's The rainbow / edited and with an introduction by
Harold Bloom.
     p. cm. — (Modern critical interpretations)
   Bibliography: p.
   Includes index.
   Contents: The rainbow : a developing rejection of old forms / Alan
Friedman — Reductive energy in The rainbow / Colin Clarke — Nature
vs. society in The rainbow / Scott Sanders — The paradoxical fall :
eternal recurrence in The rainbow / Evelyn J. Hinz — A long event
of perpetual change : The rainbow / Robert Kiely — The three angels
in The rainbow / Daniel J. Schneider.
   ISBN 1-55546-023-2 (alk. paper) : $19.95
   1. Lawrence, D. H. (David Herbert), 1885-1930. Rainbow.
[1. Lawrence, D. H. (David Herbert), 1885-1930. Rainbow.
2. English literature—History and criticism.] I. Bloom, Harold.
II. Series.
PR6023.A93R3335 1988
823'.912—dc19   87-27463
                                                               CIP
                                                               AC

Contents

Editor's Note

This book gathers together a representative selection of the best critical interpretations of D. H. Lawrence's novel *The Rainbow*. The critical essays are reprinted here in the chronological order of their original publication. I am grateful to Scott Durham and Henry Finder for their assistance in editing this volume.

My introduction is an overview of Lawrence's apocalyptic vitalism, of which *The Rainbow* is a strong representation. Alan Friedman begins the chronological sequence of criticism with a study of Lawrence's deliberate "resolution in openness" of his closure-refusing novel.

A questioning of Lawrence's vitalism, ambiguously seen as a reductive mode of energy, is attributed to *The Rainbow* itself by Colin Clarke. A more traditional dialectic, of nature against society, is traced in a different kind of ideological reading by Scott Sanders.

Evelyn J. Hinz interprets *The Rainbow* as an anti-evolutionary vision, so that eternal recurrence of an almost shamanistic kind becomes the narrative's way of belief. Lawrence's ambivalent view of marriage, desolate yet not without ultimate hope, is depicted by Robert Kiely as a crucial element in *The Rainbow*.

Daniel J. Schneider concludes this volume by investigating the unique form of *The Rainbow*, which he describes as "a psychological mimetic allegory" and as an achievement of true excellence. Certainly *The Rainbow*, for all its defects, is one of the few novels in English literature that seems worthy of comparison to the epic narratives of Tolstoy and Melville.

Introduction

Art was too long for Lawrence; life too close.
—R. P. BLACKMUR

I

As a judicial critic, R. P. Blackmur approximates the Arnold of our day. He *ranks* poets. His essay "Lord Tennyson's Scissors: 1912–1950" creates a new scriptural canon out of modern poetry in English. Class I: Yeats, Pound, and Eliot. Plenty of other classes, but all their members standing below Pound and Eliot. In a rather sad class, the violent school, lumped in with Lindsay, Jeffers, Roy Campbell, Sandburg, etc., are D. H. Lawrence and Hart Crane. Lawrence and Crane "were outside the tradition they enriched. They stood at the edge of the precipice which yawns to those who lift too hard at their bootstraps."

Presumably, Blackmur bases this judgment upon two of his own more influential essays: "D. H. Lawrence and Expressive Form" and "New Thresholds, New Anatomies: Notes on a Text of Hart Crane." Both essays will be sizable relics when most specimens of currently fashionable analysis are lost. But because they attempt so little *description* and so much value judgment they will be relics at best. By their documentation we will remember what illusions were prevalent at a particular moment in the history of taste.

Blackmur is a critic of the rhetorical school of I. A. Richards. The school is spiritually middle-aged to old; it is in the autumn of its emblematic body. Soon it will be dead. "Lord Tennyson's Scissors" is only an episode in the school's dying. But, as criticisms die so grudgingly, the essay is worth clinical attention.

Northrop Frye has recently said that all selective approaches to tradition invariably have some ultracritical joker concealed in them. A few sentences from Frye's *Anatomy of Criticism* are enough to place Blackmur's pseudodialectics as false rhetoric:

The dialectic axis of criticism, then, has as one pole the total acceptance of the data of literature, and as the other the total acceptance of the potential values of those data. This is the real level of culture and liberal education, the fertilizing of life by learning, in which the systematic progress of scholarship flows into a systematic progress of taste and understanding. On this level there is no itch to make weighty judgments, and none of the ill effects which follow the debauchery of judiciousness, and have made the word critic a synonym for an educated shrew. Comparative estimates of value are really inferences, most valid when silent ones, from critical practice, not expressed principles guiding its practice.

What I propose to do here is to examine Blackmur's "debauchery of judiciousness" in his criticism of Lawrence, and to suggest where it is inadequate to the poetry.

Poetry is the embodiment of a more than rational energy. This truth, basic to Coleridge and Blake, and to Lawrence as their romantic heir, is inimical to Blackmur's "rationally constructed imagination," which he posits throughout his criticism. Eliot's, we are to gather, is a rational imagination, Lawrence's is not. Eliot is orderly; the lines beginning "Lady of silences" in *Ash-Wednesday* convey a sense of controlled hysteria. Lawrence is merely hysterical: the concluding lines of "Tortoise Shout" are a "ritual frenzy." The great mystics, and Eliot as their poetic follower, saw their ultimate vision "within the terms of an orderly insight." But Lawrence did not. Result: "In them, reason was stretched to include disorder and achieved mystery. In Lawrence, the reader is left to supply the reason and the form; for Lawrence only expresses the substance."

The underlying dialectic here is a social one; Blackmur respects a codified vision, an institutionalized insight, more than the imaginative Word of an individual Romantic poet, be he Blake or Lawrence or Crane. In fairness to Blackmur one remembers his insistence that critics are *not* the fathers of a new church, as well as his quiet rejoinder to Eliot's *After Strange Gods:* "The hysteria of institutions is more dreadful than that of individuals." But why should the order of institutions be more valid for poetry than the order of a gifted individual? And why must order in poetry be "rational," in Blackmur's minimal sense of the word? Lawrence's poetry, like Blake's, is animate with mental energy: it does not lack *mind*. For it is precisely in a quality of mind, in imaginative invention, that Lawrence's poetry excels. Compared to it, the religious poetry of Eliot suggests everywhere an absence of mind, a poverty of invention, a reliance upon the ritual frenzy of others.

Blackmur, who is so patient an exegete of verse he admires, will not even grant that Lawrence's poetry is *worth* descriptive criticism:

> You cannot talk about the art of his poetry because it exists only at the minimum level of self-expression, as in the later, more important poems, or because, as in the earlier accentual rhymed pieces written while he was getting under way, its art is mostly attested by its badness.

Neither half of this confident judgment is true, but Blackmur has a thesis about Lawrence's poetry that he wants very much to prove. The poetry does not matter if the essay can be turned well to its despite. For Lawrence, according to this critic who denies his fatherhood in a new faith, is guilty of the "fallacy of expressive form." Blackmur's proof-of-guilt is to quote Lawrence external to his poetry, analyze the quotation, and then to quote without comment some fragments of Lawrence's verse ripped from context. But the fact is that Lawrence was a bad critic of his own poetry. Lawrence may have believed in "expressive form"; his poetry largely does not.

Blackmur quotes the final lines of "Medlars and Sorb Apples":

> Orphic farewell, and farewell, and farewell
> And the *ego sum* of Dionysos
> The *sono io* of perfect drunkenness.
> Intoxication of final loneliness.

Here, for Blackmur, "the hysteria is increased and the observation becomes vision, and leaves, perhaps, the confines of poetry." We can begin by restoring the context, so as to get at an accurate description of these "hysterical" lines. For the tone of "Medlars and Sorb Apples" is very quiet, and those final lines that Blackmur would incant as "ritual frenzy" are slow with irony, if that word is still available in the discussion of poetry. The Orphic farewell is a leave-taking of a bride left in the earth, and no frenzy accompanies it here.

"Medlars and Sorb Apples" might be called a natural emblem poem, as are most of the *Birds, Beasts and Flowers* sequence; one of the signatures of all things. In the "brown morbidity" of the medlar, as it falls through its stages of decay, Lawrence tastes the "delicious rottenness" of Orphism, the worship of the "Dionysos of the Underworld," god of isolation and of poetry. For the retorts of medlars and sorb apples distill the exquisite odor of the autumnal leave-taking of the year, essence of the parting in Hades of Orpheus and Eurydice. The intoxication of this odor, mingled with Marsala, provides that gasp of further isolation that imaginatively completes the loneliness of the individual soul. The poem is an invocation of this ultimate loneliness as the best state of the soul. The four final lines are addressed directly to medlar and sorb apples as an Orphic farewell, but different in kind from the Eurydice-parting, because of Lawrence's identification of Orpheus with Dionysos. This Orphic farewell is a creative vivification, a declaration of Dionysiac being, a perfect, lonely, intoxicated finality of the isolated self of the poet. What smells of death in the autumnal fruit is life to him. Spring will mean inevitable division, crucifixion into sex, a genuine Orphic farewell to solipsistic wholeness. The poem is resolved finally as two overlapping cycles, both ironically treated.

"Tortoise Shout" is Blackmur's prime example of "the hysteria of expression" in Lawrence, where "every notation and association, every symbolic suggestion" possible is brought to bear upon "the shrieking plasm of the self." In contrast, Eliot's Rose Garden with Virgin is our rational restorative to invocatory control.

Eliot's passage is a simple, quite mechanical catalogue of clean Catholic contradictions, very good for playing a bead-game but not much as imaginative meaning. The Virgin is calm and distressed, torn and most whole, exhausted and life-giving, etc. To Blackmur, these ritualistic paradoxes inform "nearly the same theme" as "Tortoise Shout." Unless *Ash-Wednesday* takes all meaning as its province, I am at a loss to know what Blackmur thinks he means. He invites us to "examine the eighteen pages of the poems about tortoises" with him, but as he does not do any examining, we ought perhaps to read them for ourselves.

The Tortoise poems, a continuous sequence, communicate a homely and humorous, if despairing, love for the tortoise, in itself and as emblematic of man and all created nature involved in sexual division and strife. The Tortoise-Christ identifications have throughout them a grim unpretentious joy, which Blackmur, on defensive grounds, takes as hysteria.

"Baby Tortoise," the first poem, celebrates the infant creature as Ulyssean atom, invincible and indomitable. The best parallel is Whitman, in his praise of animals who do not whine about their condition. "No one ever heard you complain." The baby tortoise is a life-bearer, a Titan against the inertia of the lifeless. But he is a Titan circumscribed by a demiurge like Blake's Urizen; this is the burden of the next poem, "Tortoise Shell," which seems to me closer to Blake than anything else by Lawrence or by Yeats. Blake's Urizen,

the Old Man of the Compasses, draws horizons (as his name and its deriva-
tion indicate). The Nobodaddy who made the Tortoise in its fallen condition circumscribes with the cross:

> The Cross, the Cross
> Goes deeper in than we know,
> Deeper into life;
> Right into the marrow
> And through the bone.

On the back of the baby tortoise Lawrence reads the terrible geometry
of subjection to "the mystic mathematics of the city of heaven." Under all
the eternal dome of mathematical law the tortoise is subjected to natural
bondage; he exhibits the long cleavage of division. An arbitrary division,
a Urizenic patterning, has been made, and the tortoise must bear it eternally.
Lawrence's earlier tone of celebration is necessarily modulated into a Blakean
and humanistic bitterness:

> The Lord wrote it all down on the little slate
> Of the baby tortoise.
> Outward and visible indication of the plan within,
> The complex, manifold involvedness of an individual creature
> Plotted out.

Against this natural binding the tortoise opposes his stoic individuality,
his slow intensity. In "Tortoise Family Connections" his more-than-human
independence is established, both as against Christ:

> He does not even trouble to answer: "Woman, what have I to do
> with thee?"
> He wearily looks the other way.

and against Adam:

> To be a tortoise!
> Think of it, in a garden of inert clods
> A brisk, brindled little tortoise, all to himself—
> Adam!

The gentle homeliness that follows, in "Lui Et Elle" and "Tortoise Gallan-
try," is punctuated by a purely male bitterness, in preparation for the great
and climactic poem of the series, "Tortoise Shout."

This last poem is central in Romantic tradition, deriving ultimately as much from Wordsworth as from Whitman. Parallel to it is Melville's enigmatic and powerful "After the Pleasure Party":

> For, Nature, in no shallow surge
> Against thee either sex may urge,
> Why hast thou made us but in halves—
> Co-relatives? This makes us slaves.
> If these co-relatives never meet
> Self-hood itself seems incomplete.
> And such the dicing of blind fate
> Few matching halves here meet and mate.
> What Cosmic jest or Anarch blunder
> The human integral clove asunder
> And shied the fractions through life's gate?

Lawrence also is not concerned with asking the question for the answer's sake:

> Why were we crucified into sex?
> Why were we not left rounded off, and finished in ourselves,
> As we began,
> As he certainly began, so perfectly alone?

The subject of "Tortoise Shout" is initially the waking of the tortoise into the agony of a fall into sexual division, a waking into life as the heretofore silent creature screams faintly in its arousal. The scream may be just audible, or it may sound "on the plasm direct." In the single scream Lawrence places all cries that are "half music, half horror," in an instructive ordering. The cry of the newborn, the sound of the veil being rent, the "screaming in Pentecost, receiving the ghost." The ultimate identity, achieved in an empathy dependent upon Wordsworthian recollection, is between the tortoise-cry in orgasm, and Christ's Passion on the Cross, the connecting reference being dependent upon the poem "Tortoise Shell."

The violence of expression here, obscene blasphemy to the orthodox, has its parallels in Nietzsche and in Yeats when they treat the Passion. Lawrence structures this deliberate violence quite carefully. First, a close account of the tortoise in coition, emphasizing the aspects of the act beyond the tortoise's single control. Then a startling catalogue (the form from Whitman, the mode from Wordsworth) of memories of boyhood and youth, before the major incantation assigned by Blackmur to the realm of the hysterical.

The passage of reminiscence works by positing a series of similitudes that are finally seen as a composite identity. The cries of trapped animals, of animals in passion, of animals wounded, animals newborn, are all resolved on the human plane as the infant's birth pang, the mother singing to herself, the young collier finding his mature voice. For all these represent:

> The first elements of foreign speech
> On wild dark lips.

The voice of the solitary consciousness is in each case modified, usually by pain, into the speech of what is divided, of what is made to know its own separateness. Here, as in Wordsworth's great "Ode," the awareness of separateness is equated to the first intimations of mortality.

The last protesting cry of the male tortoise "at extremity" is "more than all these" in that it is more desperate, "less than all these" in that it is faintest. It is a cry of final defeat:

> Tiny from under the very edge of the farthest far-off horizon of life.

One sees why Lawrence has chosen the tortoise; the horizon of separateness-in-sexual-division could not be extended further and still be manageable in a poem of this kind. From this extreme Lawrence carries us to the other pole of human similitude, Christ or Osiris being divided, undergoing ultimate dismemberment:

> The cross,
> The wheel on which our silence first is broken,
> Sex, which breaks up our integrity, our single inviolability, our
>   deep silence,
> Tearing a cry from us.
>
> Sex, which breaks us into voice, sets us calling across the deeps,
>   calling, calling for the complement,
> Singing, and calling, and singing again, being answered, having
>   found.
>
> Torn, to become whole again, after long seeking for what is lost,
> The same cry from the tortoise as from Christ, the Osiris-cry of
>   abandonment,
> That which is whole, torn asunder,
> That which is in part, finding its whole again throughout the
>   universe.

Much of the meaning of this is conveyed through rhythmical mastery; the scattering and reuniting of the self is incanted susccessively, now widening, now narrowing.

The cross here is the mechanical and mathematical body, the fallen residue of Blake's Human Form Divine. It is also the circumscribed tortoise body, as adumbrated in "Tortoise Shell." As such, the cross is a demonic image, symbolizing enforced division (into male and female, or *in* the self, or self kept from another self) and torture (tearing on the wheel, crucifixion). The tortoise, torn asunder in coming together, and perpetually caught in that cyclic paradox, utters the same cry as the perpetually sacrificed Osiris in his vegetative cycle. Christ's cry of forsakenness, to Lawrence, is one with these, as the divine nature is torn apart in the Passion. The sexual reduction in this last similitude is imaginatively unfortunate, but as interpretation does not issue from Lawrence alone.

Blackmur, defending Eliot as a dogmatic critic and poet, has written that "conviction in the end is opinion and personality, which however greatly valuable cannot satisfy those who wrongly expect more." The remark is sound, but Blackmur has been inconsistent in its application.

Lawrence, as a Romantic poet, was compelled by the conventions of his mode to present the conceptual aspect of his imagery as self-generated. I have borrowed most of this sentence from Frye's *Anatomy of Criticism,* where it refers to Blake, Shelley, Goethe, and Victor Hugo. What Frye calls a mode of literature, mythopoeia, is to Blackmur "that great race of English writers whose work totters precisely where it towers, collapses exactly in its strength: work written out of a tortured Protestant sensibility." We are back in a social dialectic external to criticism being applied to criticism. Writers who are Protestant, romantic, radical, exemplify "the deracinated, unsupported imagination, the mind for which, since it lacked rational structure sufficient to its burdens, experience was too much." This dialectic is out of Hulme, Pound, and Eliot, and at last we are weary of it. Under its influence Blackmur has tried to salvage Wallace Stevens as a late Augustan, while Allen Tate has asserted that Yeats's romanticism will be invented by his critics. That the imagination needs support can perhaps be argued; that a structure properly conservative, classical, and Catholic enough is its necessary support is simply a social polemic, and irrelevant to the criticism of poetry.

Lawrence himself, if we allow ourselves to quote him out of context, can be left to answer his judicious critic:

> What thing better are you, what worse?
> What have you to do with the mysteries

Of this ancient place, of my ancient curse?
What place have you in my histories?

Lawrence, whom the older Yeats so deeply and understandably admired, is in much of his poetry and many of his novels and polemical writings another prophet of irrationalism, but his central poems and novels are well within the most relevant aspects of the Romantic tradition and make their own highly individual contribution to the Romantic vision of a later reason. The insights of his finest novels, *The Rainbow* and *Women in Love,* are condensed in the relatively early and very Blakean *Under the Oak,* while the blind vitalism and consequent irrationalism of the later novels like *Lady Chatterley's Lover* and *The Plumed Serpent* are compensated for by the sane and majestic death-poems, like "Bavarian Gentians" and "Ship of Death," and particularly by the poem called "Shadows," which moves me as much as any verse of our century.

The speaker of *Under the Oak* is experiencing a moment of vision, a moment so intense and privileged that the whole natural context in which he stands becomes a confinement set against him, a covering that must be ripped asunder though his life run out with it. He speaks to the reader, the "you" of the poem, his rational, his too-rational companion underneath the sacrificial Tree of Mystery, and his impatience chastises our rationalizations and hesitations, our troubled refusal to yield ourselves to a moment of vision. Like Balder slain by the mistletoe, the poet is sacrificed to the chthonic forces, and struggles against a Druidic adversary, as in Blake's tradition. We are excluded, unless we too can break the barrier of natural and rational confinement:

Above me springs the blood-born mistletoe
In the shady smoke.
But who are you, twittering to and fro
Beneath the oak?

What thing better are you, what worse?
What have you to do with the mysteries
Of this ancient place, of my ancient curse?
What place have you in my histories?

At the end, Lawrence felt the full strength of that ancient curse. The marvel of his death poems is that they raise the ancient blessing of the Romantic Later Reason against the curse, the triumph over it. So, in the sublime opening of "Shadows":

> And if tonight my soul may find her peace
> in sleep, and sink in good oblivion,
> and in the morning wake like a new-opened flower
> then I have been dipped again in God, and new created.

The poem turns on an imagistic contrast between the new-opened flowers of a still-unfolding consciousness and the lengthening and darkening shadows of mortality. The imagination's antagonist in the poem is not to be found in the actual shadows but in a reasonable conception of mortality, a conception that would make what Lawrence calls "good oblivion" impossible. In a related death-poem, "The End, The Beginning," Lawrence writes:

> If there were not an utter and absolute dark
> of silence and sheer oblivion
> at the core of everything,
> how terrible the sun would be,
> how ghastly it would be to strike a match, and make a light.
>
> But the very sun himself is pivoted
> upon a core of pure oblivion,
> so is a candle, even as a match.
>
> And if there were not an absolute, utter forgetting
> and a ceasing to know, a perfect ceasing to know
> and a silent, sheer cessation of all awareness
> how terrible life would be!
> how terrible it would be to think and know, to have consciousness!
>
> But dipped, once dipped in dark oblivion
> the soul has peace, inward and lovely peace.

Renewal depends upon the expunging of self-consciousness as much as it did in "Resolution and Independence." Lawrence's death-poem "Shadows" is finally a hymn of renovation, of the privileged moments becoming "a new morning."

II

Returning, twenty-seven years later, to what is now most of the first half of this introduction, is partly a self-reminder that Lawrence no longer needs the kind of defense that he required in the 1950s, which was the age of critical formalism, when R. P. Blackmur, Allen Tate, and their precursor T. S. Eliot reigned over the world of letters. Partly the editor is also reminded that at fifty-five he is not capable of the polemical zeal he manifested at twenty-eight. The Romantic tradition has been reinstated and has its own ironical triumph. The poet Eliot is widely recognized now as one of its monuments, akin to his actual precursors, Whitman and Tennyson. And more ironically still, when I compare Blackmur and Tate to nearly any current critics, I see that Blackmur and Tate are to be praised as having more in common with Walter Pater than with my brethren.

Blackmur and Tate do not confuse poets with slumlords, as neo-Marxists do. They do not confuse poetry with post-Hegelian philosophy, do not read codes instead of poems, and do not worship a Gallo-Germano Demiurge named or troped as "Language." Unfortunately, they did mix poetry up with Eliot's version of theology, but at least they never forgot the claims of experience and of the aesthetic in itself, even though they frequently forgot that these claims took precedence over what Eliot had taught them was "the tradition." Eliot expelled Lawrence as a modern heretic in *After Strange Gods,* while confidently declaring the eminent orthodoxy of James Joyce. Lawrence was a Protestant apocalyptic, as religious as Blake, but also a personal mythmaker like Blake. If the churches are Christian, then Blake and Lawrence are not, though they are altogether religious in their visions.

Joyce, like his truest precursors, Dante and Shakespeare, was a poet of the secular world. Eliot's malign critical influence has given us the Joyce of Hugh Kenner and his disciples, for whom Joyce might as well be St. Augustine, and for whom poor Poldy is a benighted Liberal Jew, bogged in Original Sin. This is hardly the Joyce or the Poldy of Richard Ellmann and William Empson, or of the common reader. Joyce was not religious, not a believer, nor particularly fond of the Roman Catholic Church. As for Poldy, if you can still read and still believe that writers can represent persons in their books, then Poldy—gently sinful, Jewish, liberal—remains the kindest, most humane, and altogether most lovable character in modern prose fiction.

Lawrence, hardly a libertine, had the radically Protestant sensibility of Milton, Shelley, Browning, Hardy—none of them Eliotic favorites. To say that Lawrence was more a Puritan than Milton is only to state what is now finely obvious. What Lawrence shares with Milton is an intense exaltation of unfallen human sexuality. With Blake, Lawrence shares the conviction that touch, the sexual sense proper, is the least fallen of the senses, which implies that redemption is most readily a sexual process. Freud and Lawrence, according to Lawrence, share little or nothing, which accounts for Lawrence's ill-informed but wonderfully vigorous polemic against Freud:

This is the moral dilemma of psychoanalysis. The analyst sets out to cure neurotic humanity by removing the cause of the neurosis. He finds that the cause of neurosis lies in some unadmitted sex desire. After all he has said about inhibition of normal sex, he is brought at last to realize that at the root of almost every neurosis lies some incest-craving, and that this incest-craving is *not the result of inhibition and normal sex-craving.* Now see the dilemma—it is a fearful one. If the incest-craving is not the outcome of any inhibition of normal desire, if it actually exists and refuses to give way before any criticism, what then? What remains but to accept it as part of the normal sex-manifestation?

Here is an issue which analysis is perfectly willing to face. Among themselves the analysts are bound to accept the incest-craving as part of the normal sexuality of man, normal, but suppressed, because of moral and perhaps biological fear. Once, however, you accept the incest-craving as part of the normal sexuality of man, you must remove all repression of incest itself. In fact, you must admit incest as you now admit sexual marriage, as a duty even. Since at last it works out that neurosis is not the result of inhibition of so-called *normal sex,* but of inhibition of incest-craving. Any inhibition must be wrong, since inevitably in the end it causes neurosis and insanity. Therefore the inhibition of incest-craving is wrong, and this wrong is the cause of practically all modern neurosis and insanity.

To believe that Freud thought that "any inhibition must be wrong" is merely outrageous. Philip Rieff subtly defends Lawrence's weird accusation by remarking that: "As a concept, the incest taboo, like any other Freudian hypothesis, represents a scientific projection of the false standards governing erotic relations within the family." Lawrence surely sensed this, but chose to misunderstand Freud for some of the same reasons he chose to misunderstand Walt Whitman. Whitman provoked in Lawrence an anxiety of influence in regard to stance and form. Freud, also too authentic a precursor, threatened Lawrence's therapeutic originality. Like Freud's, Lawrence's ideas of drive or will stem from Schopenhauer and Nietzsche. Again like Freud, Lawrence derived considerable stimulus from later nineteenth-century materialistic thought. It is difficult to remember that so flamboyant a mythmaker as Lawrence was also a deidealizer with a reductionist aspect, but then we do not see that Freud was a great mythmaker only because we tend to believe in Freud's myths. When I was young, I knew many young

women and young men who believed in Lawrence's myths, but they all have
weathered the belief, and I do not encounter any Lawrentian believers among
the young today.

Rereading *The Rainbow* and *Women in Love* after many years, I find
them very different from what I had remembered. Decades ago I knew both
books so thoroughly that I could anticipate most paragraphs, let alone chapters,
but I too had half-believed in Lawrence, and had read as a half-believer. Now
the books seem richer and stranger, clearly an audacious and relevant myth,
and far more original than I had recalled. States of being, modes of consciousness, ambivalences of the will are represented with a clarity and vividness
that are uncanny, because the ease of representation for such difficult apprehen-
sions seems unprecedented in prose fiction. Lawrence at his strongest is an
astonishing writer, adept at saying what cannot be said, showing what cannot be shown. *The Rainbow* and, even more, *Women in Love* are his triumphs,
matched only by a few of his poems, though by many of his short stories.
In the endless war between men and women, Lawrence fights on both sides.
He is unmatched at rendering really murderous lovers' quarrels, as in chapter
23, "Excurse," of *Women in Love,* where Ursula and Birkin suffer one of
their encounters upon what Lawrence calls "this memorable battlefield":

> "I jealous! *I*—jealous! You *are* mistaken if you think that. I'm
> not jealous in the least of Hermione, she is nothing to me, not
> *that!*" And Ursula snapped her fingers. "No, it's you who are a
> liar. It's you who must return, like a dog to his vomit. It is what
> Hermione *stands* for that I *hate.* I *hate* it. It is lies, it is false, it
> is death. But you want it, you can't help it, you can't help yourself.
> You belong to that old, deathly way of living—then go back to
> it. But don't come to me, for I've nothing to do with it."
>
> And in the stress of her violent emotion, she got down from
> the car and went to the hedgerow, picking unconsciously some
> flesh-pink spindleberries, some of which were burst, showing their
> orange seeds.
>
> "Ah, you are a fool," he cried bitterly, with some contempt.
>
> "Yes, I am. I *am* a fool. And thank God for it. I'm too big
> a fool to swallow your cleverness. God be praised. You go to
> your women—go to them—they are your sort—you've always
> had a string of them trailing after you—and you always will. Go
> to your spiritual brides—but don't come to me as well, because
> I'm not having any, thank you. You're not satisfied, are you?
> Your spiritual brides can't give you what you want, they aren't

common and fleshy enough for you, aren't they? So you come to me, and keep them in the background! You will marry me for daily use. But you'll keep yourself well provided with spiritual brides in the background. I know your dirty little game." Suddenly a flame ran over her, and she stamped her foot madly on the road, and he winced, afraid that she would strike him. "And *I, I'm* not spiritual enough. *I'm* not as spiritual as that Hermione—!" Her brows knitted, her eyes blazed like a tiger's. "Then *go* to her, that's all I say, *go* to her, *go.* Ha, she spiritual—*spiritual,* she! A dirty materialist as she is. *She* spiritual? What does she care for, what is her spirituality? What *is* it?" Her fury seemed to blaze out and burn his face. He shrank a little. "I tell you, it's *dirt, dirt,* and nothing *but* dirt. And it's dirt you want, you crave for it. Spiritual! Is *that* spiritual, her bullying, her conceit, her sordid, materialism? She's a fishwife, a fishwife, she is such a materialist. And all so sordid. What does she work out to, in the end, with all her social passion, as you call it. Social passion— what social passion has she?—show it me!—where is it? She wants petty, immediate *power,* she wants the illusion that she is a great woman, that is all. In her soul she's a devilish unbeliever, common as dirt. That's what she is, at the bottom. And all the rest is pretence—but you love it. You love the sham spiritually, it's your food. And why? Because of the dirt underneath. Do you think I don't know the foulness of your sex life—and hers?—I do. And it's that foulness you want, you liar. Then have it, have it. You're such a liar."

She turned away, spasmodically tearing the twigs of spindleberry from the hedge, and fastening them, with vibrating fingers, in the bosom of her coat.

He stood watching in silence. A wonderful tenderness burned in him at the sight of her quivering, so sensitive fingers: and at the same time he was full of rage and callousness.

This passage-at-arms moves between Ursula's unconscious picking of the fleshly, burst spindleberries, open to their seeds, and her turning away, tearing the spindleberry twigs so as to fasten them in her coat. Birkin reads the spindleberries as the exposed flesh of what Freud called one's own bodily ego, suffering here a *sparagmos* by a maenad-like Ursula. It is as though Birkin himself, lashed by her language, becomes a frontier being, caught between psyche and body. Repelled yet simultaneously drawn by a sort of Orphic wonder, Birkin yields to her ferocity that is not so much jealousy as it is the woman's protest against Birkin's Lawrentian and male idealization of sexual love. What Ursula most deeply rejects is that the idealization is both flawed and ambivalent, because it is founded upon a displaced Protestantism that both craves total union and cannot abide such annihilation of individuality. Birkin-Lawrence has in him the taint of the Protestant God, and implicitly is always announcing to Ursula: "Be like me, but do not dare to be too like me!" an injunction that necessarily infuriates Ursula. Since Lawrence is both Birkin and Ursula, he has the curious trait, for a novelist, of perpetually infuriating himself.

III

Lawrence compares oddly with the other major British writers of fiction in this century: Hardy, Conrad, Kipling, Joyce, Forster, Woolf, Beckett. He is primarily a religious writer, precisely apocalyptic; they are not, unless you count Beckett, by negation. His last book, *Apocalypse,* written as he died slowly in the winter of 1929–30, begins with Lawrence remembering that his own first feeling about the Revelation of John, and indeed of the entire Bible, was negative:

> Perhaps the most detestable of all these books of the Bible, taken superficially, is Revelation. By the time I was ten, I am sure I had heard, and read, that book ten times over, even without knowing or take real heed. And without ever knowing or thinking about it, I am sure it always roused in me a real dislike. Without realising it, I must, from earliest childhood have detested the pie-pie, mouthing, solemn, portentous, loud way in which everybody read the Bible, whether it was parsons or teachers or ordinary persons. I dislike the "parson" voice through and through my bones. And this voice, I remember, was always at its worst when mouthing out some portion of Revelation. Even the phrases that still fascinate me I cannot recall without shuddering, because I can still hear the portentous declamation of a nonconformist clergyman: "And I saw heaven opened, and behold a white horse; and he that sat upon it was called"—there my memory suddenly stops, deliberately blotting out the next words: "Faithful and True." I hated, even as a child, allegory: people having the names of mere qualities, like this somebody on a white horse, called "Faithful and True." In the same way I could never read *Pilgrim's Progress*. When as a small boy I learnt from Euclid that: "The

whole is greater than the part," I immediately knew that that solved the problem of allegory for me. A man is more than a Christian, a rider on a white horse must be more than mere Faithfulness and Truth, and when people are mere personifications of qualities they cease to be people for me. Though as a young man I almost loved Spenser and his *Faerie Queene,* I had to gulp at his allegory.

Yet by the end of his book, Lawrence has allegorized Revelation into "the dark side of Christianity, of individualism, and of democracy, the side the world at large now shows us." This side Lawrence simply calls "suicide":

> The Apocalypse shows us what we are resisting, unnaturally. We are unnaturally resisting our connection with the cosmos, with the world, with mankind, with the nation, with the family. All these connections are, in the Apocalypse, anathema, and they are anathema to us. We *cannot bear connection.* That is our malady. We *must* break away, and be isolate. We call that being free, being individual. Beyond a certain point, which we have reached, it is suicide. Perhaps we have chosen suicide. Well and good. The Apocalypse too chose suicide, with subsequent self-glorification.

This would seem to be no longer the voice of Birkin, who in effect said to Ursula: "We *must* break away, and be isolate," but who never learned how to stress properly his antithetical desire for connection. Lawrence, approaching his own end, is suddenly moved to what may be his single most powerful utterance, surpassing even the greatest passages in the fiction and the late poetry:

> But the Apocalypse shows, by its very resistance, the things that the human heart secretly yearns after. By the very frenzy with which the Apocalypse destroys the sun and the stars, the world, and all kings and all rulers, all scarlet and purple and cinnamon, all harlots, finally all men altogether who are not "sealed," we can see how deeply the apocalyptists are yearning for the sun and the stars and the earth and the waters of the earth, for nobility and lordship and might, and scarlet and gold splendour, for passionate love, and a proper unison with men, apart from this sealing business. What man most passionately wants is his living wholeness and his living unison, not his own isolate salvation of his "soul," Man wants his physical fulfillment first and foremost, since now, once and once only, he is in the flesh and potent. For man, the vast marvel is to be alive. For man, as for flower and

beast and bird, the supreme triumph is to be most vividly, most perfectly alive. Whatever the unborn and the dead may know, they cannot know the beauty, the marvel of being alive in the flesh. The dead may look after the afterwards. But the magnificent here and now of life in the flesh is ours, and ours alone, and ours only for a time. We ought to dance with rapture that we should be alive and in the flesh, and part of the living, incarnate cosmos. I am part of the sun as my eye is part of me. That I am part of the earth my feet know perfectly, and my blood is part of the sea. My soul knows that I am part of the human race, my soul is an organic part of the great human soul, as my spirit is part of my nation. In my own very self, I am part of my family. There is nothing of me that is alone and absolute except my mind, and we shall find that the mind has no existence by itself, it is only the glitter of the sun on the surface of the waters.

Starting with the shrewd realization that apocalyptic frenzy is a reaction-formation to a deep yearning for fulfillment, this celebratory passage moves rapidly into an ecstasy of heroic vitalism, transcending the Zarathustra of Nietzsche and the related reveries of Pater in the "Conclusion" to *The Renaissance*. Lawrence may not have known that these were his ancestral texts in this rhapsody, but I suspect that he deliberately transumes Pater's "we have an interval, and then our place knows us no more," in his own: "But the magnificent here and now of life in the flesh is ours, and ours alone, and ours only for a time." Pater, hesitant and elaborate, skeptical and masochistic, added: "For our one chance lies in expanding that interval, in getting as many pulsations as possible into the given time." Lawrence, truly apocalyptic only in his vitalism, aligns himself rather with Whitman and Blake in refusing that aesthetic one chance, in favor of the dream of becoming integral, rather than a fragment:

What we want is to destroy our false, inorganic connections, especially those related to money, and re-establish the living organic connections, with the cosmos, the sun and earth, with mankind and nation and family. Start with the sun, and the rest will slowly, slowly happen.

IV

Lawrence died four months short of his forty-fifth birthday, with every evidence that he was making a fresh start as poet and as visionary polemicist.

As a novelist, he had suffered a decline, in the movement from the eminence of *The Rainbow* (1915) and *Women in Love* (1920) through the very problematical *Aaron's Rod* (1922) and *Kangaroo* (1923) on to the spectacular disaster of *The Plumed Serpent* (1926) and the somewhat tendentious *Lady Chatterley's Lover* (1928). Lawrence's greatest pride was in his achievement as a novelist, but it is the short novels and tales of his last decade, rather than the longer fictions, that persuade us how much was lost by his early death.

Despite the intense arguments of Dr. F. R. Leavis, Lawrence is not quite at home in any canon of the great English novelists, particularly when compared to Conrad. Even *The Rainbow* and *Women in Love* share more with Blake and Shelley, Whitman and Nietzsche, than they do with *Middlemarch* and *The Portrait of a Lady*. Beneath their narrative procedures, Lawrence's two great novels essentially are visionary prose poems, inhabited by giant forms acting out the civil wars of the psyche. In the penultimate chapter of *The Rainbow*, aptly titled "The Bitterness of Ecstasy," Ursula and Skrebensky suffer their final embrace together:

> Then there in the great flare of light, she clinched hold of him, hard, as if suddenly she had the strength of destruction, she fastened her arms round him and tightened him in her grip, whilst her mouth sought his in a hard, rending, ever-increasing kiss, till his body was powerless in her grip, his heart melted in fear from the fierce, beaked, harpy's kiss. The water washed again over their feet, but she took no notice. She seemed unaware, she seemed to be pressing in her beaked mouth till she had the heart of him. Then, at last, she drew away and looked at him—looked at him. He knew what she wanted. He took her by the hand and led her across the foreshore, back to the sandhills. She went silently. He felt as if the ordeal of proof was upon him, for life or death. He led her to a dark hollow.
> "No, here," she said, going out to the slope full under the moonshine. She lay motionless, with wide-open eyes looking at the moon. He came direct to her, without preliminaries. She held him pinned down at the chest, awful. The fight, the struggle for consummation was terrible. It lasted till it was agony to his soul, till he succumbed, till he gave way as if dead, lay with his face buried, partly in her hair, partly in the sand, motionless, as if he would be motionless now for ever, hidden away in the dark, buried, only buried, he only wanted to be buried in the goodly darkness, only that, and no more.

He seemed to swoon. It was a long time before he came to himself. He was aware of an unusual motion of her breast. He looked up. Her face lay like an image in the moonlight, the eyes wide open, rigid. But out of her eyes, slowly, there rolled a tear, that glittered in the moonlight as it ran down her cheek.

He felt as if the knife were being pushed into his already dead body. With head strained back, he watched, drawn tense, for some minutes, watched the unaltering, rigid face like metal in the moonlight, the fixed, unseeing eye, in which slowly the water gathered, shook with glittering moonlight, then surcharged, brimmed over and ran trickling, a tear with its burden of moonlight, into the darkness, to fall in the sand.

Dreadfully impressive, this possesses both the force of an experiential representation and the form of High Romantic mythology. It could be a warring coition of Blake's Los and Enitharmon, an instance of what Blake called a "Reasoning from the loins in the unreal forms of Beulah's night." Presumably Lawrence intended it as part of his prophecy against "sex in the head," but in this instance he wrought too much better, perhaps, than even he knew. The pathos of these paragraphs would be excessive, except for their mythic implications. Short as it was, life was too long for Lawrence, art too close.

The Rainbow: A "Developing Rejection of Old Forms"

Alan Friedman

From first page to last page the organization of *The Rainbow* is planned to provide, inevitably, for the absence of any conclusion. The interaction between the inner tensions of character and the outer pressures of plot, place, and pace give rise to waves or climactic movements of experience which are constantly prevented from falling and closing. The movement is always "outward" from a center, "beyond" a limit, and into the "unknown."

The novel begins with a five-page introductory passage. The first paragraph tells us that for generations each of the Brangwens had been

> aware of something standing above him and beyond him in the distance.
>
> There was a look in the eyes of the Brangwens as if they were expecting something unknown, about which they were eager. They had that air of readiness for what would come to them, a kind of surety, an expectancy.

The suggested experience of a movement which will not finally cease, the organic rhythm whose very moment of falling back is the beginning of an impulsion forward, is just as deliberately evoked for us on the second page.

> But heaven and earth was teeming around them, and how should this cease? They felt the rush of the sap in spring, they knew the wave which cannot halt, but every year throws forward the

From *The Turn of the Novel.* © 1966 by Alan Friedman. Oxford University Press, 1966.

> seed to begetting, and, falling back, leaves the young-born on
> the earth.

The anonymous Brangwen women, out of whom come the novel's three generations, looked out to the "world beyond" (the third page insists): "faced outwards" to the world of men, to "what was beyond, to enlarge their own scope and range and freedom." To a Brangwen woman, her own menfolk lacked "outwardness and range of motion," and were on this account less attractive than the vicar, who had "a range of being" (the fourth page continues to insist).

> She knew her husband. But in the vicar's nature was that which
> passed beyond her knowledge.

"The wonder of the beyond was before them," the fifth page tells us (over and over), holding out for us characters who "moved in the wonder of the beyond." As it turns out, the impulse beyond knowledge into the unknown, predicated by the introduction, is the energy which not only shapes the several arcs of experience of which *The Rainbow* consists, but determines and even makes imperative the absence of the "inevitable" conclusions of fiction. Instead of a limited conclusion, instead of a close that is knowable and hence delimiting, we are given ultimately Ursula's rejection of the known and knowable Anton Skrebensky. And the falling of the wave ("which cannot halt") is followed by the rainbow image: the pledge not only of a new world, but in effect of Ursula's union in *Women in Love* with the still unknown and unknowable Birkin.

The contrary force, the energy of closure and constriction which produces the tension out of which the novel rises, begins exactly here as the five-page introductory section ends and the narrative proper opens: a canal is constructed within a high embankment that closes off the Marsh Farm of the Brangwens from the world beyond. "So the Marsh was shut off from Ilkeston, and enclosed in the small valley bed." The novel, the inexorable struggle outward and beyond any limiting terminus, begins.

The separate stories of the three generations in *The Rainbow* are all told not merely with careful regard for, but actually in explicit terms of, openings and closings, expansion and constriction. Lydia Lensky, the Polish lady whom Tom Brangwen marries in the first chapter, represents for Brangwen, we learn, that which is foreign, unknown, and, he soon discovers, unknowable. She herself is entirely closed to life when he first meets her; it is because he compels her to open herself to him that she takes him for her second husband. For Tom Brangwen, the movement is "beyond":

he saw her hands, ungloved, folded in her lap, and he noticed the wedding-ring on her finger. It excluded him: it was a closed circle. It bound her life, the wedding-ring, it stood for her life in which he could have no part. Nevertheless, beyond all this, there was herself and himself which should meet.

As the Brangwens begin to move outward from the Marsh, a series of foreigners provides a sense of direction: a "small, withered foreigner" and his girl; Lydia Lensky; Anna Lensky; Anton Skrebensky; and ultimately (in *Women in Love*) the sculptor Loerke. (The direction of movement from the enclosed lowlands of the Marsh Farm at Ilkeston leads, as Ursula keeps remembering in the later book, to the open pinnacles of the Swiss Alps.) Even before he meets Lydia, very early in *The Rainbow,* young Tom Brangwen takes a trip by horse away from the Marsh Farm to a distant tavern.

His mind was one big excitement. The girl and the foreigner: he knew neither of their names. Yet they had set fire to the homestead of his nature, and he would be burned out of cover. Of the two experiences, perhaps the meeting with the foreigner was the more significant. But the girl—he had not settled about the girl.

He did not know. He had to leave it there, as it was. He could not sum up his experiences.

No resolution, no settling, no summing up. Only the movement out:

He balked the mean enclosure of reality, stood stubbornly like a bull at a gate, refusing to re-enter the well-known round of his own life.

That is why he marries Lydia Lensky. The marriage which "terminates" their courtship is in no sense the usual resolution of tensions, in no sense the usual containment of hitherto expanding impulses. On their wedding night, Tom Brangwen reflects:

Behind her, there was so much unknown to him. When he approached her, he came to such a terrible painful unknown. How could he embrace it and fathom it? . . . If he stretched and strained for ever he would never be able to grasp it all, and to yield himself naked out of his own hands into the unknown power! . . . What was it then that she was, to which he must also deliver himself up, and which at the same time he must embrace, contain?

The very success of their union lies in its irresolution: "he seemed to live thus in contact with her, in contact with the unknown, the unaccountable and incalculable."

The first chapter ends (as do each of the larger internal divisions of the novel) with a suggestion of the rainbow on which the last page of the book will rest.

> Then somewhere in the night a radiance again, like a vapour. And all the sky was teeming and tearing along, a vast disorder of flying shapes and darkness and ragged fumes of light and a great brown circling halo.

But the fact that the interlocking stories of the three generations simply balance, just as one story gives way to the next, on the image of the rainbow arching in the heavens, is in itself not really very impressive. It is the fact that in each case the rainbow arch is conceived as a circle half concluded, as an open circle leading out and beyond, in short as a doorway to the next generation and the next story, that gives firm evidence of Lawrence's intentions from the start to provide us finally with only tentativeness, with the absence of conclusion. (The original title, *The Wedding Ring* — the "closed circle" which Lawrence refers to on page 32 — gave way to the final title *The Rainbow*. It is no small matter that the original title might serve in a pinch as a title for the majority of novels ever written, and no accident that "a closed circle" might describe the traditional shape of the novel generally.) As the book turns to the story of Anna Lensky, we are told that Tom and Lydia

> had passed through the doorway into the further space, where movement was so big, that it contained bonds and constraints and labours, and still was complete liberty. She was the doorway to him, he to her. At last they had thrown open the doors, each to the other, and had stood in the doorways facing each other, whilst the light flooded out from behind on to each of their faces, it was the transfiguration, the glorification, the admission.

> she was the gateway and the way out, . . . she was beyond, and . . . he was travelling in her through the beyond. Whither? — What does it matter?

> [Anna's] father and mother now met to the span of the heavens, and she, the child was free to play in the space beneath, between.

In that way the story of the child Anna begins.

It "ends" a hundred pages further on, or rather it yields to the story of the child Ursula, in the same way:

> [Anna] had a slight expectant feeling, as of a door half opened. . . .
> A faint, gleaming horizon, a long way off, and a rainbow like
> an archway, a shadow-door with faintly coloured coping above
> it. Must she be moving thither? [Whither? — What does it matter?]
> Something she had not, something she did not grasp, could
> not arrive at. There was something beyond her. But why must
> she start on the journey?
>
> [At dawn] she said, "it is here." And when, at evening, the sunset
> came in a red glare through the big opening in the clouds, she
> said again, "It is beyond."
> Dawn and sunset were the feet of the rainbow that spanned
> the day, and she saw the hope, the promise. Why should she travel
> any further?
>
> With satisfaction she relinquished the adventure to the unknown.
> She was bearing her children.
> There was another child coming, and Anna lapsed into vague
> content. If she were not the wayfarer to the unknown, if she were
> arrived now, settled in her builded house, a rich woman, still her
> doors opened under the arch of the rainbow, her threshold reflected
> the passing of the sun and moon, the great travellers, her house
> was full of the echo of journeying.
> She was a door and a threshold, she herself. Through her another
> soul was coming, to stand upon her as upon the threshold, look-
> ing out, shading its eyes for the direction to take.

The "direction" of the last section of the novel, the tentativeness of the last pages, the inevitable inconclusiveness toward which Ursula's story will drive her, can hardly be imagined to be a weakening of artistry in the novel. (To conceive of the story's final direction as a sort of failure or wavering is a failure in reading or a wavering of the critical imagination; it is the triumph, that is to say, of habit.)

At Anna's wedding, directly in the middle of her story, Lawrence takes care to warn us that her stepfather, Tom Brangwen, still remembering his own wedding, was still wondering even now if he ever should feel arrived and established. He was here at Anna's wedding. Well, what right had he to feel responsible, like a father? He was still as unsure and unfixed as when he had married himself. His wife and he! With a pang of anguish he realized what uncertainties they both were.

And just in case the "direction" or the "end" which the novelist envisions for his novel should not as yet be entirely clear, he adds:

> When did one come to an end? In which direction was it finished? There was no end, no finish, only this roaring vast space. Did one never get old, never die? That was the clue.

This "clue" is embedded in the midst of a wedding ceremony, traditionally "The End" of fictional careers; and the entire meditation on how one finishes is embedded in a longer passage (too long to quote) which for two pages burns intermittently with the prismatic colors of the rainbow "whilst the heavens shimmered and roared about them." And *that* entire passage concludes:

> Always it was so unfinished and unformed!

Much the same form ("always . . . unformed") molds the story of Will Brangwen, Anna's husband. As *his* story ends, or rather as it gives place to the story of his child Ursula, we read:

> He was aware of some limit to himself, of something unformed in his very being, of some buds which were not ripe in him, some folded centres of darkness which would never develop and unfold whilst he was alive in the body. He was unready for fulfilment. Something undeveloped in him limited him, there was a darkness in him which he *could* not unfold, which would never unfold in him.

And much, much later in the novel, we learn that he was still

> in one of his states of flux. After all these years, he began to see a loophole of freedom. . . . The growing up of his daughters, their developing rejection of old forms set him also free.
>
> He was a man of ceaseless activity. Blindly, like a mole, he pushed his way out of the earth that covered him, working always away from the physical element in which his life was captured. Slowly, blindly, gropingly, with what initiative was left to him, he made his way towards individual expression and individual form.

Slowly, gropingly, but not blindly, Lawrence is creating a novel whose individual form ought not to be missed.

"The growing up of [Will's] daughters" is, as we shall see, a "developing rejection of old forms" not only for them but for their novelist. (Gudrun's rejection of old forms waits for *Women in Love.*) The never finished, "unformed" form in which Ursula's story is conceived and, it is only fair to say, fulfilled, is held before our eyes dazzlingly in *The Rainbow.* Of her mother, Anna, we have already read:

> With satisfaction she relinquished the adventure to the unknown.
> She was bearing her children.

Of Ursula (at another crucial wedding, her brother Fred's) we read:

> Waves of delirious darkness ran through her soul. She wanted to let go. She wanted to reach and be among the flashing stars, she wanted to race with her feet and be beyond the confines of this earth. She was mad to be gone.

"Why should she travel any further?" is the question her mother, Anna, asks. Ursula, we are told much later, "was a traveller on the face of the earth" and "like a bird tossed into mid-air."

One has only to consider the way in which for hundreds of pages Lawrence renders Ursula's relation to other people, and especially to Skrebensky, to see the astonishing consistency with which he sets in motion the finally unstable conclusion of her experience.

> And still [Skrebensky] had not got her, she was hard and bright as ever, intact. But he must weave himself round her, enclose her in a net of shadow, of darkness, so she would be like a bright creature gleaming in a net of shadows, caught.

> She believed that love was a way, a means, not an end in itself, as Maggie seemed to think. And always the way of love would be found. *But whither did it lead?* [Italics added.]

> Ursula suffered and enjoyed . . . Maggie's fundamental sadness of enclosedness. Maggie enjoyed and suffered Ursula's struggles against the confines of her life. And then the two girls began to drift apart, as Ursula broke from that form of life wherein Maggie must remain enclosed.

> Nay, if [Skrebensky] had remained true to her, he would have been the doorway to her, into the boundless sky of happiness and plunging, inexhaustible freedom which was the paradise of her soul. Ah, the great range he would have opened to her, the illimitable endless space for self-realization and delight for ever.

Indeed, when she and Anton made love ("She would not love him in a house any more . . . She was free up among the stars"), Lawrence's vocabulary moves in a single sentence from "clasped," "clenched," and "close" to "open" and "unfathomable":

> She took him, she clasped him, clenched him close, but her eyes were open looking at the stars, it was as if the stars were lying with her and entering the unfathomable darkness of her womb, fathoming her at last. It was not him.

And when she realizes that she will have to leave him, she thinks:

> He seemed completed now. . . . He seemed added up, finished. She knew him all round, not on any side did he lead into the unknown.
>
> "It isn't supposed to lead anywhere, is it?" said Dorothy, satirically. "I thought it was the one thing which is an end in itself."
> "Then what does it matter to me?" cried Ursula. "As an end in itself, I could love a hundred men, one after the other. Why should I end with a Skrebensky?"
>
> The trouble began at evening. Then a yearning for something unknown came over her, a passion for something she knew not what.
>
> "Well, what have I done?" he asked, in a rather querulous voice.
> "I don't know," she said, in the same dull, feeling voice. "It is finished. It has been a failure."

The word "finished" here means not only "over" but "complete," "perfected." The entire fiction which has gone before has made Ursula's point luminously clear. The narrative has taken the greatest pains to establish in its own terms that whatever is perfected or perfectable, "has been a failure"; whatever is to be perfect, must lead only into the unknown. To task Lawrence's novel with a failure to provide a finished conclusion becomes, under these circumstances, more than a trifle absurd.

The shape of "the wave which cannot halt" on page two, and the energy of the incessant quest for the unknown on page 299 ("She must leap from the known into the unknown . . . her breast strained as if in bonds"), provide, then, the energetic shape not only of Ursula's experience but of the entire fiction which her personal history "concludes." The saga of the Brangwens which begins on page one by telling us

> There was a look in the eyes of the Brangwens as if they were expecting something unknown, about which they were eager

ends when Ursula rejects Anton Skrebensky:

> He was that which is known.

That ending ("It was the unknown, the unexplored, the undiscovered upon whose shore she had landed, alone, after crossing the void") capped by the rainbow image in the last paragraphs, is more than a convenient example of an open form in fiction; it is almost a manifesto for a form that is still expanding as the novel closes. Nor is it possible to regard this energetic impulsion merely as a provision for a "sequel" in *Women in Love.* For the latter's ending is, if anything, still more of an anti-conclusion. (Both novels are "finished" works in one sense of that term; but both have expanding ends.) And in *The Rainbow* specifically, the opening end has been coming for a long time and from a long way back.

The contrary direction of energy, narrative impulses toward a desirable final restriction of experience and a "finished" conclusion, do also run through Ursula's story. Since these impulses provide a necessary tension, it is not surprising that they become more frequent and more insistent in the last chapter, *after* Ursula has rejected Skrebensky. Indeed the fossil remains of the customary novelistic "finish" in marriage and death are imprinted on the final section of the book like ghostly forms. Ursula writes to Anton, asking him to take her back and marry her; and in an extraordinary moment, just as if she herself were the novelist of her story, Ursula looks forward to "the time when she should join him again and her history would be concluded for ever."

She repents her violation of the normal course of development. "I cannot tell you the remorse I feel for my wicked, perverse behaviour." She will "live simply as a good wife to him. What did the self, the form of life, matter?" Self? Form of life? All this is of course a direct inversion of what she has thought earlier:

Self was a oneness with the infinite. To be oneself was a supreme, gleaming triumph of infinity.

And it is a direct reminder of the passage already cited, in which

Ursula broke from that *form of life* wherein Maggie must remain enclosed.

Indeed, the entire passage which stands almost at the opening of the last chapter can be read as a succinct definition of the closed form of experience in fiction, just as the present study has all along, and less succinctly, defined it. In that passage, in her penultimate decision, Ursula rejects the expanding form of the novel and bows her personal will to the force of cultural convention and literary tradition which demands a closed form for experience. (The italics below are of course mine.)

What did the self, the form of life, matter? Only the living from day to day mattered, the beloved existence in the body, rich, *peaceful, complete, with no beyond, no further trouble, no further complication.* She had been wrong, she had been arrogant and wicked, wanting that other thing, that fantastic freedom, that illusory, conceited fulfilment which she had imagined she could not have with Skrebensky. Who was she to be wanting some fantastic fulfilment in her life? Was it not enough that she had her man, her children, her place of shelter under the sun? Was it not enough for her, as it had been enough for her mother? She would marry and love her husband and fill her place simply. That was the ideal.

That is certainly the ideal, the "inevitable" conclusion. And the ideal is full of echoes: Ursula is with child, she will be "rich," she will live "in the body," in a "place of shelter," and "under the sun," as her mother, Anna, did. Quite plainly, Ursula's next-to-last choice echoes Anna's last choice in that passage which stands at the end of Anna's cycle of experience and stamps its form:

Soon, she felt sure of her husband. She knew his dark face and the extent of its passion. She knew his slim, vigorous body, she said it was hers. Then there was no denying her. She was a rich woman enjoying her riches.

And soon again she was with child. Which made her satisfied and took away her discontent. She forgot that she had watched the sun climb up and pass his way, a magnificent traveller surging forward. . . . [She was] settled in her builded house, a rich woman.

This choice then, Anna's, becomes precisely Ursula's next-to-last decision, the choice of a closed form; the parallel should indicate beyond the possibility of doubt Lawrence's coherent plan throughout the novel for the expanding form on which it closes. For Ursula, who has everywhere been shown as a "magnificent traveller surging forward," and whose travels will quite literally continue to the Alps in a later novel, cannot finally tolerate the closed ending. Her almost-final decision to be bound by Skrebensky (whom she must finally reject) drives her to a state of physical fever and mental hallucination bordering on madness.

> Why must she be bound, aching and cramped with the bondage,
> to Skrebensky and Skrebensky's world? Anton's world: it became
> in her feverish brain a compression which enclosed her. If she could
> not get out of the compression she would go mad.

This is that recurrent point in fiction, the point of fever, nightmare, despair, and disorder which we have observed in earlier chapters of this study, and which regularly signals the most intense and expanded point in the climactic form of experience in fiction. Here Ursula's moment of agonizing moral choice is accompanied by her nightmare vision of the thundering horses ("It was the crisis. . . . Then suddenly, in a flame of agony, she darted, seized the rugged knots of the oak-tree and began to climb"); and it is accompanied by delirium ("She was very ill for a fortnight, delirious, shaken and racked. . . . In her delirium she beat and beat at the question"). Regularly of course, in the form of fiction which Lawrence has all along been challenging, these moments are followed by episodes which reduce the intensity achieved and narrow the stream of conscience.

Lawrence, who has no such plans, is thus faced by a considerable problem of technique: what sort of episode can follow nightmare and delirium without reducing their intensity; what sort of episode can reduce the moral disorder while expanding the moral scope of Ursula's experience in the *same* direction as that in which it has been evolving? Given Lawrence's purposes, which are the obverse of the usual novelist's usual purposes, it is difficult to imagine a more successful solution—a resolution in openness—than Ursula's vision of the rainbow as a "finish" for the flood of experience.

As she grew better, she sat to watch a new creation.

Reductive Energy in *The Rainbow*

Colin Clarke

In *The Rainbow* as in Lawrence's work at large, the vitalistic virtues—
spontaneity, untamed energy, intensity of being, power—are endorsed
elaborately. But the endorsement is noticeably more ambiguous on some
occasions than on others. The vitality of the young Will Brangwen (he reminds
Anna "of some animal, some mysterious animal that lived in the darkness
under the leaves and never came out, but which lived vividly, swift and
intense") is one thing; the vitality that Will and Anna eventually release in
themselves in their bouts of natural-unnatural sensuality is another. So for
that matter is Ursula's fierce salt-burning corrosiveness under the moon, or
the corrupt African potency of Skrebensky. In the one instance life is affirmed
directly; positively, unambiguously, if also with potential ferocity and
violence—but in the other instances reductively, in disintegration or corruption.

Here then, one would have thought, is a distinction of some thematic
importance; yet, curiously, the final effect of the novel is to play the distinction down. The power of the horses which threaten and terrify Ursula in
the last chapter is, we sense, significantly different from the corrosive menace
of Ursula herself in the moonlight, and we feel that somehow the difference
ought to tell in the story; yet nothing is made of it. It is of course a difference-
in-similarity. In each case we are concerned with the menace of power in
unmitigated assertion and it has in fact been argued, by H. M. Daleski [in
The Forked Flame], that Ursula's traumatic adventure recapitulates symbolically
the decisive moments in her soul's journey, reenacting her past surrenders
to "the anarchy of elemental passion." But although, positioned as it is, the

From *River of Dissolution: D. H. Lawrence and English Romanticism.* © 1969 by Colin Clarke. Barnes
& Noble, 1969.

episode would appear to make some claim to summational significance, the claim is in fact only partially substantiated. If indeed, as Daleski has argued, the "pressing, pressing, pressing" of the horses refers us back to the sort of assertion to which Ursula herself had resorted with Skrebensky, a frenetic assertion of her feminine self in the endeavour to burst free to fulness of being, it must still be said that there is a great deal in her relationship with her lover to which the episode, so interpreted, has no relevance. For what has this display of massive equine power to do with the explosive life-affirmation of the Ursula who most lives in our imaginations, the corrosive-disintegrative Ursula whose affirmation of life is at the same time a reduction of life? And after all it is this paradoxical Ursula who is the growing point as well as the strength of the novel in its latter phases; it is she who points forward most emphatically to *Women in Love.*

Moreover, Ursula's corrosiveness is anticipated by her father's; the one story has its roots deep in the other. So if the significance of the later story is not caught up adequately into the final chapter, the same is true, inevitably, of the earlier one. It is the *recurrent* exploration into the reductive processes that, more than anything else, gives continuity and shape to the novel; and by the same token it is the failure to realize the full cumulative significance of the discoveries made in the course of that exploration that does most to account for one's sense, towards the end, of a richness of meaning that has not altogether found its proper form. This at any rate is the case I propose to argue in the present chapter. "The novel is the highest example of subtle inter-relatedness that man has discovered," Lawrence was to claim later. It is just this interrelatedness that we find wanting, too often, in the later half of *The Rainbow.*

In the chapter "Anna Victrix" we remark the partial emergence of a syndrome of images that was to prove crucial in the articulation of the reductive theme in *Women in Love;* and no passage is more prophetic than the following, with its ambiguous stress on enforced *downward* movement.

> At first she went on blithely enough with him shut down beside her. But then his spell began to take hold of her. The dark, seething potency of him, the power of a creature that lies hidden, and exerts its will to the destruction of the free-running creature, as the tiger lying in the darkness of the leaves steadily enforces the fall and death of the light creatures that drink by the waterside in the morning, gradually began to take effect on her. Though he lay there in his darkness and did not move, yet she knew he lay

waiting for her. She felt his will fastening on her and pulling her down, even whilst he was silent and obscure.

She found that, in all her outgoings and her incomings, he prevented her. Gradually she realized that she was being borne down by him, borne down by the clinging, heavy weight of him, that he was pulling her down as a leopard clings to a wild cow and exhausts her and pulls her down. . . .

. . . Why did he want to drag her down, and kill her spirit? Why did he want to deny her spirit? Why did he deny her spirituality, hold her for a body only? And was he to claim her carcase? . . .

"What do you do to me?" she cried. . . . "There is something horrible in you, something dark and beastly in your will."

Will's reductive activity is potent, vital, sanctioned by Nature (assimilated, that is, to the splendid destructiveness of leopards and tigers) but also debilitating, *un*-natural, monstrous. The downward tug is a degradation, an obscenity: "And was he to claim her carcase?" Whether Will is "actually" as monstrous as he seems to Anna is not of course a critical issue. There is no way of going behind the words themselves to unverbalized facts, and what the words present us with is something like an antinomy—a vision of horror and perversity imposed, immediately, upon a no less cogent vision of potency and life. What we carry away is an impression not so much of complexity of "character" as of the value-and-cost of living within the darkness.

And the same is true of the way Will's impressively rendered sensuality is directly overlaid by his agonizing sense of vacuity and dependence; he is extremely vulnerable, and at the same time powerful. This point needs to be laboured a little, because of the way the dependence and weakness have been dwelt upon in critical commentaries and the potency correspondingly ignored. Of the potency we are assured again and again:

There was something thick, dark, dense, powerful about him that irritated her too deeply for her to speak of it.

or:

And ever and again he appeared as the dread flame of power. Sometimes, when he stood in the doorway, his face lit up, he seemed like an Annunciation to her, her heart beat fast. And she watched him, suspended. He had a dark, burning being that she dreaded and resisted.

Yet Daleski permits himself to remark that Will is "the weak, if not quite the broken, end of the arch"; and he concludes that the conflict between Will and Anna "derives, ultimately, from *his* imperfections." One wonders then how it is that Anna should come in time to sustain herself with her husband's subterranean strength:

> She learned not to dread and to hate him, but to fill herself with him, to give herself to his black, sensual power, that was hidden all the daytime.

On the other hand we are not allowed to forget that the power Will mediates in the darkness is paid for by an acquaintance with the *terrors* of the darkness— and the obscenities too.

> She wanted to desert him, to leave him a prey to the open, with the unclean dogs of the darkness setting on to devour him. He must beat her, and make her stay with him.

In the paragraph immediately preceding we find this:

> And, at the bottom of her soul, she felt he wanted her to be dark, unnatural. Sometimes, when he seemed like the darkness cover- ing and smothering her, she revolted almost in horror, and struck at him.

Will is terrified of the unclean creatures of the dark; yet in Anna's eyes he is one of those creatures himself, potent, sinister, horrifying. In short, what at one moment is potency becomes at the next, with a sudden shift of perspec- tive, vulnerability. Nor are terror and horror absolute qualities—or static; they create, or convert themselves into their opposites: "*Because* she dreaded him and held him in horror, he became wicked, he wanted to destroy"; "And he began to shudder. . . . He must beat her, and make her stay with him." In both Will and Anna power is a function of vulnerability and vulnerability of power.

The reading Leavis offers then seems to me to do these scenes less than justice:

> Anna, on the face of it, might seem to be the aggressor. The rele- vant aspect of her has its clear dramatization in the scene that led to the banning of the book; the scene in which she is sur- prised by Will dancing the defiant triumph of her pregnancy, naked in her bedroom. She is the Magna Mater, the type-figure adverted to so much in *Women in Love* of a feminine dominance that must

defeat the growth of any prosperous long-term relation between a man and a woman.

But we have to recognize that this dominance in Anna has for its complement a dependence in Will. There are passages that convey to us with the most disturbing force the paradoxical insufferableness to Anna of such a dependence, and its self-frustrating disastrousness. This inability to stand alone constitutes a criticism of a positive trait of Will's towards which Anna feels a deep antipathy. In a sense that Lawrence's art defines very clearly, he is religious. It is a religiousness that provokes in Anna a destructive rationalism, and the scenes that give us the clash leave us in no doubt that both attitudes are being criticized. The whole treatment of religion in this chapter, called "Anna Victrix," which deals with it directly in a sustained way, is very subtle in its distinctions and its delicacies.

This, surely, is too rationalistic, and moralistic, to convey a full sense of the paradoxical richness of the text. Will doesn't, or shouldn't, lose marks for his inability to stand alone. What should register with us rather is the manifest weakness-in-strength; this, we have to recognize, is what it is like to be a natural inhabitant of the darkness. In other words, it is not so much that "attitudes are being criticized" as that we are being made aware of the cost of a certain kind of human experience. The potency and the capacity for degradation — the fear of the night and the splendid dark sensuality — belong to a single individual, and what is being deviously suggested is that the potency can't be had *without* the degradation. The more sophisticated strategy of *Women in Love* is already within sight.

If the endorsement of reductive power in "Anna Victrix" is largely oblique, by the time we reach the chapter "The Child" it has become explicit, though not, for that reason, unambiguous. First there is the account of Will's unconsummated seduction of the young girl he meets in Nottingham. A moralistic interpretation of this scene, entailing a simple ethical judgment on Will's perversity and pursuit of sensation for its own sake, would drastically impoverish its significance.

> He did not care about her, except that he wanted to overcome her resistance, to have her in his power, fully and exhaustively to enjoy her.

This and similar passages, taken out of context, could be used to support the view that the whole episode points the distance between a fully human sexuality and the aridness of unassimilated desire.

> Just his own senses were supreme. All the rest was external, insignificant, leaving him alone with this girl whom he wanted to absorb, whose properties he wanted to absorb into his own senses. . . .
> . . . But he was patiently working for her relaxation, patiently, his whole being fixed in the smile of latent gratification, his whole body electric with a subtle, powerful, reducing force upon her.

Yet this premeditated sensuality (one notes how often Lawrence resorts to the image of electricity to suggest the *frisson* of white or sensational sex) opens up for Will a new world of Absolute Beauty.

> And his hand that grasped her side felt one curve of her, and it seemed like a new creation to him, a reality, an absolute, an existing tangible beauty of the absolute.

Clearly, the human value of Will's experience is by no means easily determined. Indeed its final value *cannot* be determined; the effect of Lawrence's art is to discourage in the reader any tendency to reach a single and ready-defined judgment. The destruction of the flesh in conscious sensuality is presented very deliberately for contemplation, as though the intention were to invite a dismissive moral judgment; but, just as deliberately, any such judgment is held at bay. The perversity and destructiveness are fully conceded and, artistically, fully realized; but so is the beauty, the "amazing beauty and pleasure." As so often in Lawrence's work the effect is one of double exposure: we register the impulse to destruction even while we acknowledge the enhancement of life.

These complexities and tensions are sustained and indeed intensified in the sequence that follows when Will, returning home, incites Anna to a new kind of love-making, "a sensuality violent and extreme as death."

> There was no tenderness, no love between them any more, only the maddening, sensuous lust for discovery and the insatiable, exorbitant gratification in the sensual beauties of her body. . . .
> They accepted shame, and were one with it in their most unlicensed pleasures. It was incorporated. It was a bud that blossomed into beauty and heavy, fundamental gratification.

Mark Spilka's comment on these pages, in *The Love Ethic of D. H. Lawrence,* runs as follows:

They revel in one another, as Tom Brangwen and his wife had revelled before them, and as Rupert and Ursula (Brangwen) Birkin would revel after them, in order to root out all shame, all fear of the body's secrets: . . .

Here Lawrence seems to find a place, in marriage, for cold, lustful desire (as opposed, apparently, to "hot, living desire"); and its function — a limited one — is discovery and purification: a sensual revel, a phallic "hunting out" which leaves one free for the deeper, warmer love he generally upholds. But more than this, the experience sets Brangwen free to attend to his public tasks, which he had hitherto endured as so much mechanical activity. Now his purposive self is roused and released, and he begins at 30 to teach woodwork classes at the Cossethay night-school. About ten years later he returns to his own creative work in wood and other materials, and soon afterwards he receives an appointment as Art and Handwork Instructor for the County of Nottingham. Through the purgation process, both he and his wife have been aroused to active, purposive life — she, from the long sleep of motherhood; he, from social sterility to a point of social and self-respect.

And in a footnote, after quoting a comparable scene from *Lady Chatterley's Lover* ("Burning out the shames, the deepest, oldest shames, in the most secret places . . .") he adds:

What the experience does for Constance Chatterley it also does for Will and Anna Brangwen. It is a purgation process, and less the norm of love than a release to full, creative life.

This reading is faithful to the text up to a point, for Brangwen's profound sensual activity does release in him a socially purposive self. And yet what we observe first and foremost is that the new licentiousness has an absolute, or non-instrumental, value. Obviously (for the language is quite explicit) Will's sensuality is disintegrative. A deliberate, piecemeal exploitation of the body takes the place of tenderness and love. Yet this disintegrative sex is now discovered to be a way-in to life, and, above all, a revelation of beauty, "supreme, immoral, Absolute Beauty." This is the bold truth we are required to confront; and Spilka's reading tends to dissipate it. It is the final paragraphs of the chapter that that reading is most relevant to, for there we find ourselves in a more reassuring, not to say cosy world, where social purposiveness is triumphant and even lust turns (eventually) a moral mill.

> He wanted to be unanimous with the whole of purposive mankind.
> . . . For the first time, he began to take real interest in a public affair. He had at length, from his profound sensual activity, developed a real purposive self.

The *rapprochement* effected between the reductive and the creative in these last paragraphs impresses one as willed and glib, indeed as largely unreal. We are not to be convinced by mere assertion that social purposiveness can develop out of sensuality and a profound moral indifference; this, surely, is something that calls for patient demonstration.

On the other hand the "mere assertion" was in itself an achievement; Lawrence was breaking new ground, even if he was doing so at a purely discursive level. To gauge the distance, as it were, between the "argument" of the paragraphs under review and the "argument" of the paragraphs that conclude the preceding chapter, "The Cathedral," is one way of enforcing this point.

> He still remained motionless, seething with inchoate rage, when his whole nature seemed to disintegrate. He seemed to live with a strain upon himself, and occasionally came these dark, chaotic rages, the lust for destruction. She then fought with him, and their fights were horrible, murderous. And then the passion between them came just as black and awful. . . .
> He made himself a woodwork shed, in which to restore things which were destroyed in the church. So he had plenty to do: his wife, his child, the church, the woodwork, and his wage-earning, all occupying him. If only there were not some limit to him, some darkness across his eyes! . . .
> . . . He was unready for fulfilment. Something undeveloped in him, there was a darkness in him which he *could* not unfold, which would never unfold in him.

This might well seem to be more honest than the conclusion to the chapter that follows; for Will's lust for destruction, of which we have heard so much and which we now recognize as a basic fact about him, is not lost sight of at all, even while we are being assured of his constructiveness and purposiveness. In other words, the creative and the reductive coexist throughout; the one is not simply *substituted* for the other, as in the later passage, which seems by comparison a good deal too smooth. On the other hand the theme of the later passage is intrinsically more "difficult." Whereas in the earlier instance Will's creativeness and destructiveness, if undissociated are also causally unconnected, in the later instance it is actually *from* the destructiveness (in this case disintegrative sensuality) that the creativeness, we are to believe, proceeds, or develops. In cold fact however, the total failure to dramatize this development means that the destructive and the creative seem no more inwardly affiliated than they were in the earlier sequence. Indeed less so; virtually they lose contact.

And it is a loss of contact of just this kind that we frequently remark in the remaining chapters. The story repeatedly concerns itself with disintegration and destructiveness; and we can scarcely fail to assume, as we proceed, that it will be part of this concern to discover and define a significant pattern of relationships between *kinds* of disintegration: *this* disintegrative process will prove to have a bearing on *that*. But in the event no such pattern emerges; "cross-reference" seems both to be encouraged and not encouraged. There is the fiercely corrosive and violently destructive activity of Ursula in the moonlight; there is the corruption and social disintegration of Wiggiston, and the corresponding despair of Ursula herself—("She had no connexion with other people. Her lot was isolated and deadly. There was nothing for her anywhere, but this black disintegration"); there is the splendid-sinister potency of Skrebensky, corrupt, fecund, destructive ("He kissed her, and she quivered as if she were being destroyed, shattered"); and there is Ursula's vision of advancing corruption at the very end of the novel. But to what extent these kinds of disintegration bear upon each other is not clear. Whereas in *Women in Love* the densely reticulated imagery is constantly persuading us to see identities in difference, to make discriminations and discover analogies, in the latter part of *The Rainbow* we seem to be invited teasingly to embark on this same procedure only in the end to be frustrated.

But these judgments require substantiating and I turn first to the scene, in the chapter "First Love," in which the adolescent Ursula annihilates her lover under the moon. Once again (as in the case of Will Brangwen, "the sensual male seeking his pleasure") we find ourselves acknowledging a value in activity patently opposed to the creative and integrative. "But hard and fierce she had fastened upon him, cold as the moon and burning as a fierce salt . . . seething like some cruel, corrosive salt." "Cold . . . and burning": the oxymoron (a common one wherever Lawrence is concerned with the reductive processes) focusses the sense of an inverse vitality running counter to growth and to warm organic blood desire. Nowhere in the novel is human personality reduced more obviously and more drastically to the inhuman and inorganic, and yet nowhere are we more aware of power and energy humanly mediated. The recurrent images—moonlight, steel, corrosive salt, the sea—

exclude the organic entirely, and one thinks of the famous letter on Marinetti and the Futurists (June 5, 1914):

> It is the inhuman will, call it physiology, or like Marinetti — physiology of matter, that fascinates me. I don't so much care about what the woman *feels* — in the ordinary usage of the word. That presumes an *ego* to feel with. . . . You mustn't look in my novel for the old stable *ego* of the character.

In a stimulating article "The Narrative Technique of *The Rainbow*," Roger Sale has considered the literary means by which Lawrence contrived to "break down 'the old stable ego of character.' " It is not so much Sale's argument itself that concerns me here as the significance of that metaphor of "breaking down."

> The simplest declarative sentence is one of the main aids the novelist has in building up a stable ego, an identity. . . .
>
> If we turn to a passage in *The Rainbow,* we can show how Lawrence tries there to break down this natural building-up process.

The phrasing could not be more apt — or revealing; for "breaking down" is a common Laurentian synonym for "reduction." So Sale pays his tribute unconsciously to the iconic power of Lawrence's art, and demonstrates indirectly that the major novels are about the reductive process not only in the most obvious or literal sense but in the further sense that they themselves image that process. In the episode under review we remark how the fiercely corrosive activity of the fictive Ursula is matched, and to that extent endorsed, by the corrosive activity — no less vigorous — of the artist himself. And this endorsement goes far towards explaining why our moral sense should fail to be outraged by Ursula's "enormous wilfulness." Her attitude to Skrebensky is inhuman, but then so is the novelist's art, in the sense that part of what he is engaged in is the reduction of human personality to an inhuman or material substratum. But this involves no diminishing of artistic intensity; indeed it has the reverse effect, and the novelist creates a notable artificial beauty — a beauty "immoral and against mankind."

Probably the best gloss on these pages is a passage that I have already quoted from "The Crown." (It is a passage significant also for the kind of bearing it does *not* have on the episode or on the novel generally, as I shall argue later.)

> Leonardo knew this: he knew the strange endlessness of the flux

of corruption. It is Mona Lisa's ironic smile. Even Michael Angelo knew it. It is in his *Leda and the Swan*. For the swan is one of the symbols of divine corruption with its reptile feet buried in the ooze and mud, its voluptuous form yielding and embracing the ooze of water, its beauty white and cold and terrifying, like the dead beauty of the moon, like the water-lily, the sacred lotus, its neck and head like the snake, it is for us a flame of the cold white fire of flux, the phosphorescence of corruption, the salt, cold burning of the sea which corrodes all it touches, coldly reduces every sun-built form to ash, to the original elements. This is the beauty of the swan, the lotus, the snake, this cold white salty fire of infinite reduction. And there was some suggestion of this in the Christ of the early Christians, the Christ who was the Fish.

The paradoxes are a good deal sharper in the novel than in the essay (with the exception of that last equation of Christ and Fish), for the obvious reason that Ursula, a human being, is further removed than snake or swan from "the original elements," so that in the novel the reductive process is that much more spectacular. For all that, we are not more interested in the morality of Ursula's behaviour, essentially, than we would be in the behaviour of swan or snake. Or, to make the point perhaps less provocatively, we are interested in the morality of her behaviour only to the extent that we are interested in her dehumanization. It is relevant to recall that remarkable passage in E.T.'s memoir where an account is given of three occasions on which Lawrence became wildly distraught—possessed—under the combined influence of moonlight and sea:

> I was really frightened then—not physically, but deep in my soul. He created an atmosphere not of death which after all is part of mortality, but of an utter negation of life, as though he had become dehumanized.
>
> (E.T. [Jessie Chambers], *D. H. Lawrence, A Personal Record*)

Analogously, in the scene in *The Rainbow*, one is impressed not so much by Ursula's will to separateness, or her frenetic feminine assertiveness, though these qualities are doubtless evident enough, as by her intimidating inhumanness. Yet the further she departs from the warmly living the more evidence she gives of vitality of a different kind—inverse, disintegrative. Inverse is Birkin's word; and indeed his notion of "inverse process" is loosely relevant to the whole episode.

> When the stream of synthetic creation lapses, we find ourselves
> part of the inverse process, the blood of destructive creation.
> Aphrodite is born in the first spasm of universal dissolution—
> then the snakes and swans and lotus—marsh-flowers—and Gudrun
> and Gerald—born in the process of destructive creation. . . . It
> is a progressive process—and it ends in universal nothing.

The process can end only in a reassimilation to the anonymous energies of
nature; yet it is productive of a deadly and distinctive beauty. And in *The
Rainbow,* likewise, beauty is a product of the reductive process, a function
of reductive power.

> She stood for some moments out in the overwhelming luminosity
> of the moon. She seemed a beam of gleaming power. She was
> afraid of what she was. Looking at him, at his shadowy, unreal,
> wavering presence a sudden lust seized her, to lay hold of him
> and tear him and make him into nothing. Her hands and wrists
> felt immeasurably hard and strong, like blades.

This revelation of life and beauty where we might scarcely be supposed to
expect it, in a process that brutally affronts our sympathies—in a progressive
departure from the human—is what the episode is centrally about. (It is for
the most part a fully realized rhetorical beauty and rhetorical life, though
there is, surely, some overwriting.) To identify with Ursula's daytime consciousness, and accept as self-validating the slow horror she experiences as
she gradually recovers herself (as one critic has done) is clearly inappropriate.
Primarily, Ursula's horror is there to measure the recession of the magical
and mythic. There is no suggestion that the familiar order of reality is the
more valid or true; it is simply different.

And indeed the sheer fact of difference is stated as cogently as could
well be. It is a question however whether the statement is not in fact too
cogent. I have suggested, apropos of the final paragraphs of the chapter "The
Child," that Lawrence's task is to communicate a sense of the distinction
between pure creation and destructive creation—or the vital and the perversely
vital—without effecting a simple dissociation between them. In the earlier
sequences involving Tom and Lydia, and Anna and Will, the constant modula-
tion from the mythic to the commonplace, and vice versa, has established
the existence of a consciousness at once distinct from our familiar daytime
consciousness and at the same time prone to assert itself in the context of
daytime living. Will's murderously reductive activity in the chapter "Anna
Victrix" is a quality of his everyday behaviour and also the utterance of a

self that can seem at moments extravagantly alien. But from the stackyard scene on there is a tendency for the magical and the everyday—the subterranean self and the social self—to move apart. And the abrupt dissociation of personae at the end of the scene, when Ursula repudiates her "corrosive self" with horror (while the night is suddenly "struck back into its old, accustomed, mild reality") is, in this connection, only too suggestive of what is to come. A truth is enforced, but at the expense of a counter-truth; Ursula's ruthless energy is made to seem *merely* alien.

It is Skrebensky's character however that tends most conspicuously to bifurcate, and in a way that bears even more suggestively on my argument. If it is a mistake to interpret Ursula's lurid behaviour under the moon with a moralistic bias, it is a parallel mistake to ignore the corrupt vitality of her lover and to write him off as a hollow man *simpliciter*. Leavis has perhaps led the way here; at any rate he has concerned himself exclusively with Skrebensky's shortcomings, laying stress upon his "good-citizen acceptance of the social function as the ultimate meaning of life" and pointing to the connection between this acceptance and his "inadequacy as a lover." Others, designedly or not, have followed suit. S. L. Goldberg lumps Skrebensky with Winifred Inger and Tom Brangwen, "the irrevocably lost." Daleski, quoting the argument between Ursula and Skrebensky about being a soldier, comments:

> This passage establishes not only that Skrebensky is "not exactly" a soldier, but that he is not exactly anything. If, unlike Will, he does not deny the outside world, he accepts his place in it with a mechanical and unadventurous complacency. . . .
>
> Skrebensky is even less defined as a man than either Tom or Will; lacking the rooted stability of the one and the passionate aspiration of the other, he has no real identity.

But what of the Skrebensky who, like Ursula herself, can be a vehicle of intense vitality, positive-reductive, potent, corrupt?

> He talked to her all the while in low tones about Africa, conveying something strange and sensual to her: the negro, with his loose, soft passion that could envelope one like a bath. Gradually he transferred to her the hot, fecund darkness that possessed his own blood. He was strangely secret. The whole world must be abolished. . . .
>
> He seemed like the living darkness upon her, she was in the embrace of the strong darkness. He held her enclosed, soft,

unutterably soft, and with the unrelaxing softness of fate, the
relentless softness of fecundity. . . .

It was bliss, it was the nucleolating of the fecund darkness.
Once the vessel had vibrated till it was shattered, the light of consciousness gone, then the darkness reigned, and the unutterable
satisfaction.

Here again is that effect of double exposure to which I have already alluded:
on the one hand an impression of cultural and organic regression, on the
other hand the sensual transfiguration, "the unutterable satisfaction." It is
the familiar paradox:

"Corruption will at last break down for us the deadened forms,
and release us into the infinity."

The image of the turgid African night is parallel to those other images of
potency-in-disintegration, the flaring moon and the salt-burning sea. Skrebensky's sensuality is at once reductive, regressive, a breaking down ("One breathes
it, like a smell of blood," "The whole world must be abolished") and a release
into infinity. The sensual ecstasy has its roots in corruption. The lovers inhabit
an "unblemished darkness"; yet the matrix (as it were) of this darkness is
that other, sinister darkness of Africa. This latter is the darkness that sus-
tains them, ultimately — as the swan has its reptile feet buried in the ooze
and mud. We are in the world of *Women in Love*. The teeming night is
recognizably Birkin's "dark river of dissolution": "massive and *fluid* with
terror," "his loose, soft passion that could envelop one like a *bath*," "they
walked the darkness beside the massive *river*," "the soft *flow* of his kiss . . .
the warm fecund flow of his kiss," "one fecund nucleus of the *fluid* darkness."
This is very obviously in the spirit of the later novel. It anticipates Birkin's
"*fountain* of mystic corruption."

Yet the Ursula-Skrebensky story, it is commonly agreed, is not, by a
long way, as coherent or compelling as for the most part the story of *Women
in Love* is. And one reason at least is plain. The final movement of *The Rainbow* is organized around a single human relationship. Inevitably this deprives
Lawrence of the scope he needed for elaborating those paradoxical themes
which, all the evidence goes to show, were now so deeply engaging his
imagination. It is no accident that the single pair of lovers became two pairs
of lovers in the sequel; they had to. Skrebensky is called on to discharge the
functions of both Birkin *and* Gerald, to "figure," in Jamesian phrase, the
possibilities both for life *and* death in reductive sexuality. Not surprisingly
he proves unequal to the task. At a non-narrative level the paradox about

living disintegration can be developed and protracted as far as ingenuity will allow; but at the narrative level the limits to this process are stricter. *The Rainbow* is a novel, with a story. Skrebensky cannot, in the story, be given over finally to disintegration and also be redeemed. And, in the event, under these novelistic pressures his character falls apart into *two* characters.

On the one hand there is Skrebensky the darkly potent lover, inhabitant of the fecund universal night.

> Everything he did was a voluptuous pleasure to him—either to ride on horseback, or to walk, or to lie in the sun, or to drink in a public-house. He had no use for people, nor for words. He had an amused pleasure in everything, a great sense of voluptuous richness in himself.

There is little doubt that we are to accept this vitality as real. Moreover it entails a certain correlative distinction at a more personal and conscious level.

> She took him home, and he stayed a week-end at Beldover with her family. She loved having him in the house. Strange how he seemed to come into the atmosphere of her family, with his laughing, insidious grace. They all loved him, he was kin to them. His raillery, his warm, voluptuous mocking presence was meat and joy to the Brangwen household. For this house was always quivering with darkness, they put off their puppet form when they came home, to lie and drowse in the sun.

The emphasis here is still on the dark under-life; yet laughing insidious grace, raillery, warmth and voluptuous mockery also suggest less esoteric qualities—more "human" and social—and a corresponding fulness or completeness of being. At any rate we are left in no doubt of the richness and abundance of life which the relationship with Skrebensky, for all its limitations, does release. The lovers are held together *only* in the sensual subconsciousness, yet that only includes so much.

> Then he turned and kissed her, and she waited for him. The pain to her was the pain she wanted, the agony was the agony she wanted. She was caught up, entangled in the powerful vibration of the night. The man, what was he?—a dark, powerful vibration that encompassed her. She passed away as on a dark wind, far, far away, into the pristine darkness of paradise, into the original immortality. She entered the dark fields of immortality.

In the face of this and similar passages it is scarcely adequate to say of Skrebensky that though he satisfies Ursula "time after time in their physical relations, he fails her at the last in the 'beyondness of sex' . . . . where Birkin
in *Women in Love* will not fail with Ursula later." Something like this, it
is true, is Ursula's own reading of the situation:

> The salt, bitter passion of the sea, its indifference to the earth,
> its swinging definite motion, its strength, its attack, and its salt
> burning, seemed to provoke her to a pitch of madness, tantaliz-
> ing her with vast suggestions of fulfilment. And then, for per-
> sonification, would come Skrebensky, Skrebensky, whom she
> knew, whom she was fond of, who was attractive, but whose
> soul could not contain her in its waves of strength, nor his breast
> compel her in burning, salty passion:

But we remember not only how she and Skrebensky had "stood together,
dark, fluid, *infinitely* potent, giving the living lie to the dead whole which
contained them" or had passed away "into the pristine darkness of paradise,"
or how "perfectly and supremely free" they were, "proud beyond all question, and *surpassing mortal conditions,*" but also the sinister African potency,
the destructiveness and indifference to humanity which Skrebensky had darkly
communicated and which, I have argued, are analogous to the "salt, bitter
passion" which, we now learn, he is utterly deficient in.

But then of course there is the other Skrebensky.

> His life lay in the established order of things. He had his five senses
> too. They were to be gratified. . . .
>
> The good of the greatest number was all that mattered. That
> which was the greatest good for them all, collectively, was the
> greatest good for the individual.

This is the Skrebensky the commentators have fixed upon—a vacuity; a mere
social integer, essentially without identity and living in pure externality through
the senses.

It is true that the contrast between the two Skrebenskys is not always
as steep as the passages quoted might suggest. There are moments when the
vacuity and the power live together convincingly, are accepted as belonging
to a single person.

> He seemed so balanced and sure, he made such a confident presence.
> He was a great rider, so there was about him some of a horseman's
> sureness, and habitual definiteness of decision, also some of the

horseman's animal darkness. Yet his soul was only the more wavering, vague. . . . She could only feel the dark, heavy fixity of his
animal desire. . . . [A]ll must be kept so dark, the consciousness
must admit nothing. . . . He was always side-tracking, always
side-tracking his own soul. She could see him so well out there,
in India—one of the governing class, superimposed upon an old
civilisation, lord and master of a clumsier civilisation than his own.

Here Skrebensky's limitations are a believable aspect of his strength; the animal
darkness, the fixity of animal desire, the disinclination to bring things to
consciousness, the side-tracking of his own soul—this all hangs together.
If his soul is wavering and vague, if he virtually has no soul, this is not because
he lives purely in the senses, but because he has the inarticulateness of an
animal—both its dark power and its heavy fixity.

And if Skrebensky's sensual being impresses us as far shallower on some
occasions than on others, something similar is true of Ursula. She however
is always exempted from adverse judgment.

Yet she loved him, the body of him, whatever his decisions might
be. . . . She caught his brilliant, burnished glamour. Her heart
and her soul were shut away fast down below, hidden. She was
free of them. She was to have her satisfaction.

We may compare this with the earlier comment on Skrebensky: "He had
his five senses too. They were to be gratified." But whereas in the one instance
dissociated sensuality releases a glow and splendour of life ("She became
proud and erect, like a flower, putting itself forth in its proper strength")
in the other it is a token of death ("Skrebensky, somehow, had created a
deadness around her, a sterility, as if the world were ashes. . . . Why did
he never really want a woman, not with the whole of him: never love, never
worship, only just physically want her?"). When Skrebensky finally fails
Ursula at the end, they are engaged in a pursuit of just that kind of satisfaction
which she herself had set up as a goal ("Her heart and soul were shut away.
. . . She was to have her satisfaction"); yet responsibility for this failure seems
to be laid exclusively at Skrebensky's door.

She liked it, the electric fire of the silk under his hands upon her
limbs. . . . Yet she did not feel beautiful. All the time, she felt
she was not beautiful to him, only exciting. She let him take her,
and he seemed mad, mad with excited passion. But she, as she
lay afterwards on the cold, soft sand, looking up at the blotted,

faintly luminous sky, felt that she was as cold now as she had
been before.

The transfiguration in the flesh which Ursula had unquestionably enjoyed
with Skrebensky is here repudiated, and the intoxication of the senses which
they shared is conceived of as having ended in itself; it involved, apparently,
"no connexion with the unknown." But the reader's recollections, as I have
suggested, are different from Ursula's, and are not so rapidly erased.

One can conceive easily enough of an ending to the novel which would
seem to resolve these warring tensions: Ursula, looking back in gratitude
to the very real satisfaction and fulfilment Skrebensky had brought, might
yet acknowledge that in the end the sensual ecstasy could not in itself sustain
her. Yet, clearly, tensions as powerful as these are not to be resolved so neatly
and rationally. For Lawrence is under an evident compulsion to make *incompatible* statements about voluptuousness or dissociated sensuality, and is struggling to find a novelistic pattern sufficiently flexible to allow him to do so.
The pattern to which he is committed is transparently *not* sufficiently flexible; so we find him asserting of Skrebensky that his sensuality ends in sensuality
and yet also that it leads into the unknown.

There is an essay of this period, "The Lemon Gardens" (it appeared in the
English Review in September 1913), in which this doubleness of attitude to
self-conscious sensuality is articulated with especial clarity.

> This is the soul of the Italian since the Renaissance. In the sun-
> shine he basks asleep, gathering up a vintage into his veins which
> in the night-time he will distil into ecstatic sensual delight, the
> intense, white-cold ecstasy of darkness and moonlight, the raucous,
> cat-like, destructive enjoyment, the senses conscious and crying
> out in their consciousness in the pangs of the enjoyment, which
> has consumed the southern nation, perhaps all the Latin races,
> since the Renaissance. . . .
>
> This is one way of transfiguration into the eternal flame, the
> transfiguration through ecstasy in the flesh. . . . And this is why
> the Italian is attractive, supple, and beautiful, because he wor-
> ships the Godhead in the flesh. We envy him, we feel pale and
> insignificant beside him. Yet at the same time we feel superior to
> him, as if he were a child and we adult.
>
> Wherein are we superior? Only because we went beyond the
> phallus in the search of the Godhead, the creative origin. And
> we found the physical forces and the secrets of science. . . .

But we have exhausted ourselves in the process. We have found great treasures, and we are now impotent to use them. So we have said: "What good are these treasures, they are vulgar nothings." We have said: "Let us go back from this adventuring, let us enjoy our own flesh, like the Italian." But our habit of life, our very constitution, prevents are being quite like the Italian. The phallus will never serve us as a Godhead, because we do not believe in it: no Northern race does. Therefore, either we set ourselves to serve our children, calling them "the future," or else we turn perverse and destructive, give ourselves joy in the destruction of the flesh.

"Perverse and destructive": the tone is distinctly unsympathetic. "This is one way of transfiguration into the eternal flame": the tone is far from unsympathetic. Yet the topic is essentially the same on each occasion. True, the Italian's worship of the Godhead in the flesh is genuine, whereas the northerner's is derivative and mechanical. Yet the theme in each instance is the self-consciousness of the flesh, destructive enjoyment, the pursuit of maximum sensation, the senses conscious and crying out in their consciousness. And these in effect are the ambiguities of the Ursula-Skrebensky story. We may compare:

She vibrated like a jet of electric, firm fluid in response. Yet she did not feel beautiful. All the time, she felt she was not beautiful to him, only exciting.

And

But the fire is cold, as in the eyes of a cat, it is a green fire. It is fluid, electric.

In the essay the cold fire has a splendour absent from the episode in the novel.

This is the supremacy of the flesh, which devours all, and becomes transfigured into a magnificent brindled flame, a burning bush indeed.

But as I have suggested, a dismissive note — corresponding to the "not beautiful . . . only exciting" of the novel — is there in the essay too, in the unsympathetic attitude to the northerner's merely mechanical sensation-hunting.

And so it is that the character of Skrebensky fails in the last analysis to cohere. He is made a butt, like the northerner, because he seeks the destruction of the flesh, or pure gratification through the senses; yet just the capacity to live through the flesh, reductively, like the Italian, is his strength. It is only with *Women in Love* that Lawrence finds for this teasing paradox an appropriate dramatic correlative.

In the passage from "The Crown" which I have chosen as epigraph to the second part of this book Lawrence lists various alternative modes of the activity of departure. These are decay, corruption, destruction, and breaking down; and elsewhere in the essay he supplies others—resolving down, reduction, corrosion, decomposition, dissolution, disintegration. In *Women in Love* these various processes—in all their ambiguity as opposite equivalents of creation—are represented comprehensively; but in *The Rainbow* much less so. Decay and corruption, crucial images in the later novel, play a minor and for the most part unobtrusive role in the earlier one; moreover their value or force is not on the whole ambiguous. In the passage in which they are most obviously deployed—the account of Ursula's visit to Wiggiston with Winifred Inger—their significance is all on the surface and noticeably uncomplicated. The marsh, in *Women in Love* foul and deadly yet also a source of perverse but genuine vitality, is here merely foul and deadly. Or very nearly so.

> Her Uncle Tom too had something marshy about him—the suc-
> culent moistness and turgidity, and the same brackish, nauseating
> effect of a marsh, where life and decaying are one.

The nausea is absolute and uncomplicated, it would seem; yet even here there is a hint of the ambivalence to come.

> She too, Winifred, worshipped the impure abstraction, the
> mechanisms of matter. There, there, in the machine, in service
> of the machine, was she free from the clog and degradation of
> human feeling.

The notion that to be human is necessarily to be nourished in *corruption* ("clog and degradation") is well within sight here, so that a cross-reference to the dominant contextual image of the marsh at any rate *begins* to be set in motion: we seem to catch at some such implied significance as that the marsh, admittedly clogging and vile, is for all that, or rather all the more for that, a source of life. The resonance is faint and apparently accidental, but prophetic of *Women in Love,* without question.

In the handling of this theme of corruption in *The Rainbow* one is indeed haunted by a sense of half-realized significance. There is the treatment of Ursula's uncle Tom for instance. Before the meeting at Wiggiston he had already made a decisive impact upon her imagination, when she saw him at the farm after the drowning of his father.

She could see him, in all his elegant demeanour, bestial, almost corrupt. And she was frightened. She never forgot to look for the bestial, frightening side of him, after this.

He said "Good-bye" to his mother and went away at once. Ursula almost shrank from his kiss, now. She wanted it nevertheless, and the little revulsion as well.

And we remember this when he appears next, at the wedding (the passage is too long to quote in full).

A kind of flame of physical desire was gradually beating up in the Marsh. . . . Tom Brangwen, with all his secret power, seemed to fan the flame that was rising. . . .

The music began, and the bonds began to slip. Tom Brangwen was dancing with the bride, quick and fluid and as if in another element, inaccessible as the creatures that move in the water. . . . One couple after another was washed and absorbed into the deep underwater of the dance.

"Come," said Ursula to Skrebensky, laying her hand on his arm. . . .

It was his will and her will locked in a trance of motion, two wills locked in one motion, yet never fusing, never yielding one to the other. It was a glaucous, intertwining, delicious flux and contest in flux.

The dichotomies of the moralist are hopelessly irrelevant here. The underworld over which the half-sinister Tom Brangwen presides is a place of dangerous licence, of enchantment, of heightened life, a place for the privileged to enter. Yet if here, in his equivocal way, Tom releases life, and later, at Wiggiston, is an unequivocal agent of death, nothing is made of this duality; it generates no significance. There is no ironic juxtaposition of his two roles, as there would be in *Women in Love*; we are not manoeuvred into adopting, simultaneously or nearly so, conflicting attitudes to corruption or decay.

The final paragraphs of the novel, which are commonly acknowledged to be unconvincing, bear upon my argument with especial force. There is a demonstrable confusion of imagery in these paragraphs, amounting in fact to a sort of trickery—but of a kind that shows Lawrence feeling his way towards the richer effects of *Women in Love*.

She knew that the sordid people who crept hardscaled and separate on the face of the world's corruption were living still. . . . She saw in the rainbow the earth's new architecture, the old, brittle

corruption of houses and factories swept away, the world built
up in a living fabric of Truth, fitting to the over-arching heaven.

The hardness that Ursula discovers around her is both the hardness of death
and a hardness that conceals new life. We are asked to believe that the one
kind of hardness can become or virtually *is* the other, and on grounds that
appear to be little more than verbal. "The terrible corruption spreading over
the face of the land" is *hard, dry, brittle;* and equally hard, dry and brittle is
the "horny covering of disintegration," "the husk of an old fruition" in which
Ursula can observe "the swelling and the heaving contour of the new ger-
mination." Lawrence insists on the completeness and seeming finality of the
corruption—it is "triumphant and unopposed"—and yet it is in the very extremity of the corruption that consolation is discovered. If organisms have
everywhere disintegrated almost to dust, so much the better. The more dust-
like, the more easily "swept away"! Some such spurious logic would seem
to be implied, surely, in the collocation of "swept away," "brittle corruption" and "disintegration," and even if this were not so, one's other objection would remain: the hardness of corruption ("corruption so pure that it
is hard and brittle") cannot be translated by mere verbal sleight-of-hand into
the hardness of the husk that encloses new life.

In any case, we are left with the impression that corruption is merely
antithetical to this new life—an impression that quite fails to correspond with
the fact that the novel has been moving towards the discovery that corruption can also energize and renew. The sequence in which this movement
is most emphatic is that concerned with Skrebensky's sinister African sensuality, where, as we have seen, the language affirms both the menace of
corruption and its life-giving potency. (The concept of corruption is not
invoked explicitly in the passage, but it is clearly within call; the African
night is at once hot and fluid, and there is a powerful suggestion of over-
abundant growth.) In the novel as a whole however, the movement in question, the tendency towards a simultaneous affirmation of corruption and
vitality, is at least as much promise as realization.

> Awful and threatening it was, dangerous to a degree, even whilst
> he gave himself to it. It was pure darkness, also. All the shameful
> things of the body revealed themselves to him now with a sort
> of sinister, tropical beauty. All the shameful natural and unnatural
> acts of sensual voluptuousness which he and the woman partook
> of together, created together, they had their heavy beauty and
> their delight. Shame, what was it? It was part of extreme delight.

> It was that part of delight of which man is usually afraid. Why afraid? The secret, shameful things are most terribly beautiful.

There is not much horror in these tropics, obviously. "Sort of" necessarily deprives "sinister" of some of its force, and the analogy in any case is only a glancing one (by contrast one thinks of the African sequence, later, and of that very real Negro "with his loose, soft passion"). In short, while the beauty and the energizing power of corruption (or something like corruption) are made sufficiently real, the alternative possibilities of ugliness and nausea tend to be distanced. And though this is a strategy that might appear to be locally justified, in the larger perspective it begins to look suspect. For it is in keeping with the too-easy translation of the reductive impulses into the constructive which I have already commented on apropos of the conclusion of this episode, and to that extent contributes significantly to the relative disorganization of the novel in its latter phases.

And in this respect even the African sequence suffers, excellent as it is in itself; it too is more or less dissociated. For instance, no attempt is made to relate Skrebensky's African corruption to the no less lurid corruption at Wiggiston; and yet at one level, with his belief in the priority of social values and the unimportance of the individual, Skrebensky is heading straight for that "disintegrated lifelessness of soul" which Uncle Tom (the Wiggiston colliery-owner) and Winifred Inger, Ursula's teacher, so patently embody.

> She saw gross, ugly movements in her mistress, she saw a clayey, inert, unquickened flesh, that reminded her of the great prehistoric lizards. One day her Uncle Tom came in out of the broiling sunshine heated from walking. Then the perspiration stood out upon his head and brow, his hand was wet and hot and suffocating in its clasp. He too had something marshy about him—the succulent moistness and turgidity, and the same brackish, nauseating effect of a marsh, where life and decaying are one.

"Prehistoric," "marshy," "turgidity": it is very like the African jungle. Yet there is no particular reason why we should recall this passage, when Skrebensky's splendid-corruptive African potency is later established.

Nor does the disintegration at Wiggiston bear as suggestively as it might upon Ursula's disintegrative or destructive attitude to that disintegration. Nor for that matter is her destructive social attitude sharply enough related to the destructive violence she directs against Skrebensky. S. L. Goldberg makes a comment that is relevant here.

> Of course [Lawrence] criticizes [Ursula's] mistakes, her *affaires*
> with inadequate values, her immature, inarticulate thrashings
> about. On the other hand, however, her underlying attitudes,
> her "good heart" as it were, escape criticism altogether. Her
> characteristic Luddite reaction to industrialism, for instance, ranges
> from impotent fury to tearful sentiment, but it is never critically
> placed; nor is the equally sentimental violence that catches, in the
> surrounding darkness, at the gleam of savage animal eyes, of
> flashing swords of overpowering "angels," like fangs, "not to be
> denied." The wholesale destructiveness she unleashes on Skrebensky
> is just this radical, apocalyptic mood in action. And what is
> remarkable is not her adolescence, but Lawrence's readiness to iden-
> tify himself with her.

This is only partly acceptable; for the destructiveness Ursula unleashes on Skrebensky has a far more ambiguous value than the pure "apocalyptic" destructiveness implicit in her attitude to society. So it cannot just be said that the one *is* the other. However, a valid point remains: there is certainly an identity in the difference. Yet not enough is done to help us to an awareness either of the difference or of the identity: Lawrence's grasp on the relationship is not a fully inward one.

These are the kinds of dissociation then that characterize the latter part of the novel. For all that, Lawrence is travelling perceptibly in these pages towards the tauter organization of *Women in Love,* a work in which the notion that "life and decaying are one" is a shaping presence throughout.

Nature vs. Society in *The Rainbow*

Scott Sanders

Lawrence always stressed the nature in human nature. Like birds and wildflowers, his characters are prey to the forces and subject to the laws of the natural order. Whereas realism in the English novel before him had generally emphasized men's social experience and historical context, he stressed men's physical experience and natural context. There were precedents, to be sure, in Emily Brontë and Hardy, both of whom served him as models, and in such Naturalists as George Moore (and of course Zola in France and Dreiser, Crane, London and Norris in the United States); but none of his predecessors had ventured so deep into the unconscious in search of the natural man. Already in his first three novels nature frames and measures personal relationships. In *Sons and Lovers,* as we have seen, Paul justifies his actions by appeal to instinct; with his women he speaks in a language of natural things, of flowers and moons and trees. Only in the love-making scene by the flooded river Trent, however, where the lovers descend from the "ordinary level" of the "public path" to mingle their passion with that of the river, does Lawrence explicitly oppose the realm of flesh and flowers to the realm of social existence; and even this degree of opposition is largely due, as I have suggested, to his individualistic focus: it expresses indifference towards society rather than hostility.

At the end of that novel Paul felt isolated, adrift; although immersed in the world he "had no place in it." Lawrence himself sensed the need, in the absence of God and community, for membership in some order which transcends the individual. In a letter of December 1914, while he was in the

From *D. H. Lawrence: The World of the Five Major Novels.* © 1973 by Scott Sanders. Viking, 1974.

midst of revising *The Rainbow* for the last time, he announced that he no longer accepted the belief that " '*I* am all. All other things are but radiation out from me,' " preferring now "to try to conceive the whole, to build up a whole by means of symbolism, because symbolism avoids the I and puts aside the egotist; and, in the whole, to take our decent place." The whole in which man is to take his decent place is not society but nature, which Lawrence conceived in religious terms; individuals in *The Rainbow* are integrated into an encompassing natural process which in turn is opposed to society. Paul's need for transcendence is thus answered, but not his need for community.

I. Nature in Man

The rendering of human passion within the sympathetic embrace of a natural landscape is one of the most striking features of *The Rainbow*. Reading about Tom's courtship of Lydia, about the sheaf-gathering ballet of Will and Anna, or about the wind-swept climax of the love-affair between Ursula and Skrebensky, one feels that here Lawrence's genius is distinctly at work. By giving this last passage a closer look, we can identify certain of the linguistic means which Lawrence used to shift the focus of living and loving from society to nature:

> He came to her finally in a superb consummation. It was very dark, and again a windy, heavy night. They had come down the lane towards Beldover, down to the valley. They were at the end of their kisses, and there was the silence between them. They stood as at the edge of a cliff, with a great darkness beneath.
>
> Coming out of the lane along the darkness, with the dark space spreading down to the wind, and the twinkling lights of the station below, the far off windy chuff of a shunting train, the tiny clink-clink-clink of the wagons blown between the wind, the light of Beldoveredge twinkling upon the blackness of the hill opposite, the glow of the furnaces along the railway to the right, their steps began to falter. They would soon come out of the darkness into the lights. It was like turning back. It was unfulfilment. Two quivering, unwilling creatures, they lingered on the edge of the darkness, peering out at the lights and the machine-glimmer beyond. They could not turn back to the world—they could not.
>
> So lingering along, they came to a great oak-tree by the path. In all its budding mass it roared to the wind, and its trunk vibrated in every fibre, powerful, indomitable.

"We will sit down," he said.

And in the roaring circle under the tree, that was almost invisible yet whose powerful presence received them, they lay a moment looking at the twinkling lights on the darkness opposite, saw the sweeping brand of a train past the edge of their darkened field.

Then he turned and kissed her, and she waited for him. The pain to her was the pain she wanted, the agony was the agony she wanted. She was caught up, entangled in the powerful vibration of the night. The man, what was he? — a dark, powerful vibration that encompassed her. She passed away as on a dark wind, far, far away, into the pristine darkness of paradise, into the original immortality. She entered the dark fields of immortality.

When she rose, she felt strangely free, strong. She was not ashamed — why should she be? He was walking beside her, the man who had been with her. She had taken him, they had been together. Whither they had gone, she did not know. But it was as if she had received another nature. She belonged to the eternal, changeless place into which they had leapt together.

Her soul was sure and indifferent of the opinion of the world of artificial light. As they went up the steps of the foot-bridge over the railway, and met the train-passengers, she felt herself belonging to another world, she walked past them immune, a whole darkness dividing her from them. When she went into the lighted dining-room at home, she was impervious to the lights and the eyes of her parents. Her everyday self was just the same. She merely had another, stronger self that knew the darkness.

This curious separate strength, that existed in darkness and pride of night, never forsook her. She had never been more herself. It could not occur to her that anybody, not even the young man of the world, Skrebensky, should have anything at all to do with her permanent self. As for her temporal, social self, she let it look after itself.

Through passion Ursula gains access into the immense powers of nature. Like the adept of Zen Buddhism, her isolate, conscious self is extinguished in nature, to be replaced by a new self which participates in this larger ordering. Thus she escapes the creeping *anomie* which had overcome Paul Morel. No longer merely daughter or student or teacher, she is something at once more rudimentary and more grand, a physical creature, a nexus of vast and incomprehensible forces. Every major character in *The Rainbow* comes eventually to this realization, by way of sexuality or otherwise, for in the world of Lawrence's fiction this is the customary rite of initiation.

The love-encounter takes place in literal and semantic obscurity. The dark has edges; the night is heavy, palpable. Within the enveloping darkness the feeble lights and sounds of society merely emphasize the surrounding gloom. Beldover itself, with its spawn of industrial squalor, is swallowed in the blackness. Ursula and Skrebensky are absorbed along with the oak into the "powerful vibration of the night." Feeling themselves, like Paul and Clara, "blind agents of a great force" they cease for the moment to exist as isolate, self-directing individuals and become phases or nodes of a larger vibration.

The process of reification which we detected in *Sons and Lovers* has thus reached a more advanced state in *The Rainbow*. Loss of self-control recurs in the experience of every figure in the novel. People are possessed by demons, they lapse into spells, drown in floods; they are overcome by speechlessness, absorbed into fields of force, bewitched by the moods and motions of the natural world. All through history, Lawrence informs us in his Preface to *Movements in European History* (1921), men have been the puppets of their instincts; our comings and goings merely express the powerful forces at work in the unconscious, and therefore the nineteenth-century positivists were deluded in seeking a rational history. History is a joke which nature plays on society.

In *The Rainbow* nature invariably dwarfs society, which appears remote, frail and hostile. Ursula and Skrebensky dread returning to the "machine glimmer"—that industrial, urban, political and public world which Mellors in *Lady Chatterley's Lover* would think of bitterly as "that sparkling electric Thing outside there." Society becomes the enemy. No more will Ursula respect "the opinion of the world of artificial light," precisely because it is artificial, a small clearing feebly lit by the arc lamp of human consciousness, regulated by science, but surrounded by wild beasts wheeling in darkness. (One detects in Ursula's defiance a revolt against the Nonconformist puritanism of Mrs Lawrence. Appropriately enough, the National Purity League, which took censorship action against *The Rainbow* in 1915, was headed by a man who was, like Mrs Lawrence, a Congregationalist.) Not only are most of Lawrence's love-encounters transferred physically to another environment—to woods, moors, rivers, clearings and beaches—they are also transferred ethically into another framework of values. The old framework lingers, however, as an implicit code against which his characters revolt. It abides here in the notion of shame, in the world's opinion, in the established order of the home, in the eyes of train passengers and parents.

When Ursula returns to the world of artificial light it is the discovery of the range of her own physicality, her immersion in "the whole darkness," which distinguishes her from the uninitiated train passengers. Darkness, at first an aspect of the physical atmosphere, no more than a black space, an absence, through which a train's headlight can sweep, comes to stand for the wondrous domain of sexual experience. Thus Lawrence transforms landscape into emotional terrain (the gloomy meadows surrounding Beldover became "the dark fields of immortality"), a transformation he effects so often that we begin to doubt whether the division between inner, psychic world, and outer, natural world is really valid. By such means he assimilates Ursula's emotional state to the natural environment, and divorces both from society. Paul and Clara also defy social mores in their lovemaking beside the flooded Trent, but in their case the opposition to society remains conventional — the breaking of sexual taboos. Whereas here in the relationship between Ursula and Skrebensky the opposition has become radical. Nature and society represent wholly different systems of value, and offer wholly different grounds for identity.

Like the feeble lights engulfed by darkness, Skrebensky's four irrelevant words only intensify the silence. Human speech seems inadequate or unnecessary. Here as in the entire novel there is little correspondence between what the characters feel and what they can say about those feelings. Like his master Tolstoy, whose *Anna Karenina* lay behind both *The Rainbow* and *Women in Love,* Lawrence had an uncanny ability for depicting the nonverbal communication between people, as we have already observed in the silent speech between Mrs Morel and her son. Riffling through the pages, one is struck — in contrast to a novel by Austen or George Eliot or James — by the scarcity of dialogue, by the disparity between speech and inner life (a disparity which Henri Bergson during the same years was incorporating into a fashionable metaphysic). Lawrence's characters are often inarticulate by nature, yet many of the intense emotional states and complex psychological processes which lie outside their range of speech lie outside the range of all common speech. Venturing into a linguistic no man's land, he had to blaze his own trails. T. S. Eliot's complaint in the *Four Quartets* (account taken for differences of temperament) might apply to Lawrence as well:

> And so each venture
> Is a new beginning, a raid on the inarticulate
> With shabby equipment always deteriorating
> In the general mess of imprecision of feeling.
> Undisciplined squads of emotion.

"Darkness"—the appropriate leitmotif for a book which challenged the Enlightenment confidence in reason and language—refers not only to that in human experience which is irrational but to that which is *unsayable*. Yet a scene such as the present one is an invasion of the darkness: Lawrence has brought to the experience all the tools of the novelist. What his characters could not have said, he has written. Thus while he attacked Freud's mythology of psychic processes, because it pretended to articulate the "darkness" of the unconscious, and thereby advanced the imperialistic claims of reason, Lawrence himself was busily subduing the disorderly instincts to speech.

Description of human physicality had at the time when Lawrence was writing small space in the established uses of language. Of course the animality of *homo sapiens* had been for some time at the center of scientific speculation about man, whether one considers the biology of Darwin, Huxley and Haeckel, the sociology of Wilfred Pareto (with his notion of animal "residues"), the anthropology of Frazer, or the psycho-mythology of Freud himself. In *The Ego and the Id* Freud tells us he borrowed the German form of the id (*das Es*) from Nietzsche, who used it in a similar sense to designate "whatever in our nature is impersonal and, so to speak, subject to natural law." Nietzsche, the advocate of Dionysos, glimmers through Lawrence's prophetic writings, as he glimmers through the products of his generation. Thus Lawrence's claim for recognition of man's animality was by no means a lonely cry.

The passage which we have been considering, which is typical of his writing in this respect, gives us the impression that he was struggling to extend the boundaries of language, to encompass more of man's purely physical experience. The repetitions and restatements suggest a halting, circling attempt to grasp an experience which for Ursula is unprecedented. The progression from "dark . . . vibration" to "dark wind," to "pristine darkness of paradise," to "original immortality" and finally to "dark fields of immortality" suggests a mind driven in a frantic search for an adequate expression of an intense but verbally elusive experience, even as that experience unfolds. With Bergsonian fidelity to the contour of emotion, the text records the effort towards articulation—like the chisel-marks left in stone by Michelangelo, the texture of brush-strokes on a canvas by Van Gogh. The writing proceeds, both in individual scenes and in the whole novel, with its layered structure of generations, by what might be called bracketing, as that word is used in artillery: he fires short, long, to one side, then to the other, constantly in search of the proper range, each shot, each formulation refining slightly our perception of the target.

But the ultimate experience eludes the verbal chase. For Lawrence it was a matter of principle—and of vivid personal experience—to maintain that human physicality finally evades the reach of language, like a fox, footloose in wilderness. To have presented this love-encounter with the syntactic cat's-cradles of late James, with Flaubert's razored diction, or with the Byzantine mythologism of Joyce would have been to assert the dominion of the verbal and the conscious over the wordless and unconscious life of the body. A passage of the sort we have been considering marks the boundary of articulation, where Lawrence's most distinctive powers as a novelist were concentrated.

Nature is speechless, society verbal. The life of the "social self" is communicable in ordinary language, that of the "permanent self" is not. The contrast between nature and society coincides with the division between silence and language:

| NATURE | natural self | body | SILENCE |
| CULTURE | social self | mind | LANGUAGE |

In *The Rainbow* every comparison between the two dimensions awards precedence to nature. Man is first of all a physical creature — only derivatively is he a creature of society or history. Ursula and Skrebensky's past, their communal relations, all that pertains to their "social" selves is irrelevant to their experience: they have been led to this conclusion by the logic of their emotions. They are subjected for the moment wholly to the experience, and to the natural forces which through their sexuality they apprehend.

The opposition between society and nature is one of the dominant structuring principles of the novel. For the Brangwens society is an alien order which drives its railroads and digs its canals into the Marsh Farm; an alien world which Tom visits on market days; to which Will is only tenuously connected (even then after long indifference) by his craft instruction; and which Ursula first enters, then spurns, as a teacher. One is born into nature — one must join society. The social self is defined by the ethical and linguistic conventions of society, but the natural self is grounded in experiences which trespass those conventions. The attitude of indifference towards society in *Sons and Lovers* becomes one of defiance in *The Rainbow,* and in *Women in Love* one of horror. From *The Rainbow* onward the antagonism between social and natural man was to remain one of the dominant features of Lawrence's thought.

He was especially preoccupied with this psychological split in his wartime essays, notably the "Study of Thomas Hardy," "The Crown," "Education of the People" and "Democracy." In the latter, referring at one point to a female character in an American novel, he formulates the split in borrowed Freudian terms:

The *ego* is obviously a sort of second self, which she carries about with her. It is her body of accepted consciousness, which she has inherited more or less ready made from her father and grandfathers. This secondary self is very pernicious, dictating to her issues which are quite false to her true, deeper, spontaneous self, her creative identity.

Nothing in the world is more pernicious than the *ego* or spurious self, the conscious entity with which every individual is saddled. He receives it almost *en bloc* from the preceding generation, and spends the rest of his life trying to drag his spontaneous self from beneath the horrible incubus. And the most fatal part of the incubus, by far, is the dead leaden weight of handed-on ideals.

Although he conflates superego and ego here, his meaning is clear: the social self, bearer of community consciousness, player of social roles, is false, pernicious, spurious; the natural self, spontaneous and creative, precedes and transcends the community, it blossoms from a wholly different stratum of being. Skrebensky, Harby, Tom Jr. and Maggie Schofield represent a type of person whom Lawrence sees as given over partly or wholly to the mechanical second self. Psychoanalysts have consistently distinguished this social self, the being-in-the-world, from some primary natural self. For Freud of course the socially-imposed self was the superego; for Jung it was the *persona;* for Wilhelm Reich the "character defense structure;" and for R. D. Laing the "false-self system." Lawrence's own view was closest to that of Reich, who considered the social self a crippling and vicious imposition upon the spontaneous, animal self.

In terms of Marx's anthropology, Lawrence was much more interested in natural man than in species man, in the biological substratum than the specifically human. Marx's own emphasis was precisely the opposite—which accounts in part for Lawrence's impatience with the political and economic preoccupations of the socialists. Yet the root of his concern was not so different from that of Marx; both were spurred to criticize society by outrage over the condition of industrial workers. The criticism which was implicit in *Sons and Lovers* becomes explicit in *The Rainbow* in Lawrence's remarks on the miners of Wiggiston:

Like creatures with no more hope, but which still live and have passionate being, within some utterly unliving shell, they passed meaninglessly along, with strange, isolated dignity. It was as if a hard, horny shell enclosed them all.

The shell, the false self, has been imposed by the industrial system; the passionate being, the natural self, remains hidden within. At the end of the novel Ursula envisions a time when in each person the true natural self will burst through its shell and industrial civilization be swept away. Whereas for Marx the cause of suffering and dehumanization among workers was a particular form of society, a particular organization of industry, for Lawrence in his more extreme moments industry itself, society in whatever form, appears as the devil to be damned.

In its radical form the psychological split becomes schizoid. We can recognize many of Ursula's traits in Laing's description, in *The Divided Self*, of schizoid vacillation between intensive self-consciousness and the desire to become invisible, dissolved, "a passive thing penetrated and controlled by the other." Her craving to annihilate Skrebensky may be viewed in Laing's terms as the defense mechanism of an "ontologically insecure" person, so uncertain of her own identity that she must destroy the other or reduce him to the status of an object, for fear of disintegrating under the impact of his personality. Lawrence's tendency to see only two possibilities for the self—either complete isolation or complete merging—is one of the key features of the schizoid personality. However, as both the title and argument of Wylie Sypher's book *Loss of the Self in Modern Literature and Art* suggest, Ursula's radical uncertainty about her identity may be schizoid but it is also one of the characteristic ailments of our century. Proliferating bureaucracy, increasing urbanization, industrialization, mobility and division of labor have widened the gap between public and private selves. Robert Musil's man without qualities, Franz Kafka's anonymous Joseph K., Beckett's bodiless voices, exhibit the plight of the individual who is alienated from all forms of community, and who is also unable to identify himself in relation to any transcendent order, whether biological or theological. We have identified the beginnings of Lawrence's own social alienation in *Sons and Lovers*, his déclassement and his experience of industry as the hostile imposition of some external authority. Dissatisfied with society, therefore, in *The Rainbow* he recommends nature for his transcendent order.

II. EFFECTS OF THE UNCONSCIOUS IN EVERYDAY LIFE

Like the writings of Freud, *The Rainbow* had an unsettling effect on Lawrence's contemporaries, for it described, even celebrated, the violent eruption of the unconscious into the tranquil pastures of ordinary life. Consider for example this hectic interlude in the marriage of Tom and Lydia:

> And he remained wrathful and distinct from her, unchanged outwardly to her, but underneath a solid power of antagonism to her. Of which she became gradually aware. And it irritated her to be made aware of him, as a separate power. She lapsed into a sort of sombre exclusion, a curious communion with mysterious powers, a sort of mystic, dark state which drove him and the child nearly mad. He walked about for days stiffened with resistance to her, stiff with a will to destroy her as she was. Then suddenly, out of nowhere, there was connection between them again. It came on him as he was working in the fields. The tension, the bond, burst, and the passionate flood broke forward into a tremendous, magnificent rush, so that he felt he could snap off the trees as he passed, and create the world afresh . . . he felt a stupendous power in himself, of life, and of urgent, strong blood.

By exaggerating emotions Lawrence renders inexplicable what we normally accept as vicissitudes of love. Such terms as "wrathful," "solid power of antagonism," "mad," "stiffened with resistance," "will to destroy," "passionate flood" and "stupendous power" magnify and thereby mystify the fluctuations which attend all human relationships. People once again appear as the passive objects of their emotions: "Then suddenly, out of nowhere, there was connection between them again. It came on him." Imagined during a period of stormy relations with Frieda, as we can judge from contemporary letters and from the volume of poetry *Look! We Have Come Through!*, all the man-woman relationships in *The Rainbow* oscillate according to their own eccentric, unpredictable periods, between the poles of union and division, love and hate, tenderness and anger, in a manner reminiscent of *Anna Karenina*. By this oscillation Lawrence suggests, in a way rarely achieved, the inevitable and mysterious day-to-day mutations in love.

To register the impact of turbulent emotions he frequently disrupts syntax, as the Expressionist painters distorted the image and exaggerated line. Thus of Will Brangwen:

> If he relaxed his will he would fall, fall through endless space, into the bottomless pit, always falling, will-less, helpless, nonexistent, just dropping to extinction, falling till the fire of friction had burned out, like a falling star, then nothing, nothing, complete nothing.

In refusing to yield to the unconscious he resembles Skrebensky, who is willing to surrender himself to his nation but not to his passion. For their fear of the darkness, for their refusal to yield, both men are condemned: Skrebensky as a complete failure, Will, after his bout of sensual initiation with Anna, as but a partial success. For Will religious ecstasy takes the place of sexual ecstasy. In the account of his response to Lincoln Cathedral we again encounter distortion of syntax and parody of coital rhythms:

> Here the stone leapt up from the plain of earth, leapt up in a manifold, clustered desire each time, up, away from the horizontal earth, through twilight and dusk and the whole range of desire, through the swerving, the declination, ah, to the ecstasy, the touch, to the meeting and the consummation, the meeting, the clasp, the close embrace, the neutrality, the perfect, swooning consummation, the timeless ecstasy. There his soul remained, at the apex of the arch, clinched in the timeless ecstasy, consummated.

Words and phrases succeed each other according to the logic of metaphoric association and synonymy, rather than the logic of syntax. The hypnotic repetition so characteristic of Lawrence has the effect not only of impressing upon the reader certain key terms, but also, like slow-motion in the film, of retarding the action and focusing our attention on certain intense emotional states. Thus he distinguishes stylistically between inner or psychological time—what Bergson called *la durée*—and the outer chronometric time of science. As in the sheaf-gathering scene between Will and Anna, or the scene in which stampeding horses frighten Ursula, rhythmic repetion appears to break down the linear-temporal sequence, and to expand the moment in an hallucinatory way, evoking what Lawrence liked to call the "fourth dimension" (a term perhaps culled from newspaper accounts of Einstein's theory of general relativity, which was published in 1915, the same year as *The Rainbow*).

Psychic eruptions are commonly represented in the novel by the sort of linguistic features we have been observing: syntax is disrupted; characters are transformed into objects; qualities of feeling are hypostatized as autonomous processes ("surge," "flow," "wind"); words lose their cognitive meanings in combination ("one fecund nucleus of the fluid darkness"); repetition and metaphoric association displace syntactic relations; certain words recur like a tic or an obsession; and the rhythms of phrases suggest coitus rather than speech. Such words as "swoon," "hypnotized," "lapsed," "spell" and "possessed" crop up continually, announcing loss of self-control to overwhelming forces which are "dark" and "unknown" in that their sources are buried in the unconscious. Throughout *The Rainbow* the ordinary experiential world, which the mind seems to control and language to describe, is threatened by another order of experience, before which the mind yields and language fails.

The intensity which Lawrence infuses into these extraordinary experiences would be dissipated by ordinary speech, and so his characaters hold their peace; but theirs is not an impoverished silence, like that of Beckett's figures, the silence of the overly-conscious. Their reticence masks an excess of experience rather than a dearth. Most of what the narrator tells about their inner life could not be told by the characters themselves. I have suggested that this is mainly a consequence of Lawrence's attitude towards his material: he refused to subordinate the ungovernable and fathomless order of nature to the control of language. But it is also partly a consequence of the native inarticulacy of the characters themselves. Choosing to create people who by his measure were closer to the physical springs of life, Lawrence at the same time chose men and women who were incapable of saying much about those springs. For them the realms of darkness and silence correspond.

From the "passionate flood" which bears him along, Tom receives a sense of power, a sense of connection with some violent force—the power which Ursula discovers in the "vibration of the night," in the cell nucleus, in the stampeding horses, in moonlight; which Anna during her pregnancy identifies as the procreative Lord; which Will experiences as the thrusting hand of God. Indeed the world of *The Rainbow,* like the paintings and compositions of the Futurists, whose manifestoes Lawrence read while revising his novel, is saturated with power. People seem to dwell in a field of force, interacting with each other and with their environment through "will," "influence," "presences," "spells," "impulses," "trances," "power," "electricity" or "magnetism"—the metaphors mixing the occult with physics. We are presented with a dynamic model of man and nature (in the best tradition of nineteenth-century science) in which the conscious, self-directing individual is connected, through myriad modes of force, with his fellows and his surroundings. The dynamic model becomes even more prominent in *Women in Love,* and it is worked out with intricate physiological detail in *Psychoanalysis and the Unconscious* (1919–20) and *Fantasia of the Unconscious* (1921). Although social forces exist in the world of *The Rainbow*—as manifested with appalling cruelty in industrial Wiggiston and in Ursula's school—the more powerful forces are natural. In *Women in Love*—mainly, I believe, on account of the World War—the balance shifts in the opposite direction. History, the public world, becomes a nightmare from which the characters, like Stephen Dedalus in *Ulysses,* are trying to wake.

Lawrence's creatures inhabit an unstable world. Violent forces lurk just below the surface of consciousness. "Psychology has split and shattered the idea of a 'Person,'" E. M. Forster wrote in 1939, "and has shown that there is something incalculable in each one of us, which may at any moment rise to the surface and destroy our normal balance." The creator of the Marabar Caves, brooding on the eve of another world war, recognized that depth-psychology had undermined faith in the isolate, conscious individual, whose impulses were wholly accessible to introspection — in short, had discredited the central tenet of bourgeois ideology, around which, as Ian Watt has shown in *The Rise of the Novel,* the novel form crystallized. Simultaneously with Proust and Joyce and Gide and Hesse, but after his own fashion, Lawrence was reconceiving the person in fiction. In a well-known letter of 1914 to Edward Garnett he wrote that

> you mustn't look in my novel for the old stable *ego* — of the character. There is another *ego,* according to whose action the individual is unrecognisable, and passes through, as it were, allotropic states which it needs a deeper sense than any we've been used to exercise, to discover are states of the same single radically unchanged element.

Identity, which had appeared so stable a commodity in George Eliot, Jane Austen, Dickens and even Hardy, had become unstable — subjected from the outside to violent social forces, from the inside to the powerful beasts of the unconscious. Lawrence had come to feel that the image of the coherent, conscious self depicted by almost all previous English novelists (Laurence Sterne and Emily Brontë are major exceptions, and they stand therefore outside all formulations of the "Great Tradition"), was, as Bergson pointed out, merely a fiction which served to make sense of the flux of experience. He was less interested in the social self, the "stable ego," than in the animal self immersed in nature. Depth-psychology, with its questioning of reason and its emphasis upon the impersonal forces at work on the individual, an emphasis shared by the new science of sociology, was among the most powerful influences at that time behind the artistic experiments of Picasso and Kandinsky, the attempts at expressionism in music by Schoenberg, and the crisis in epistemology which preoccupied Weber in sociology, Einstein in physics and Russell and Wittgenstein in philosophy.

Lawrence's work stands in the midst of this reorientation of thought about the role of consciousness and the nature of identity. Among his novels *The Rainbow* marks the decisive shift in his thinking from the individualistic focus of *Sons and Lovers* to the animistic and finally religious perspective of his mature writings.

What I have called Lawrence's bracketing procedure — his movement by metaphor, synonymy, repetition, approximation — is exhibited on a broader scale in the narrative structure of *The Rainbow* itself. In the movement from generation to generation (perhaps owing something to *Buddenbrooks,* which Lawrence had read by 1913) there is a progressive widening of the terms of reference and a broadening of consciousness on the part of the characters, as there is a physical movement away from the isolated Marsh Farm into the industrial city. But despite this genuine expansion of the novel's world, despite its passage from the agrarian nineteenth century to the urban twentieth, each of the three successive generations restates essentially the same set of problems: the attempt to define a man-woman relationship that will be mutually fulfilling; the struggle for a sense of self that does not depend upon the domination of other people; the search for a compromise between the claims of nature and the claims of society. Not every generation achieves the same degree of success in solving these problems, but every generation undergoes very much the same trials. The rhythms of courtship, sexual initiation, struggle between man and woman, violent oscillations in love, and experimental encounters with the social world, recur in the life of every major figure in the novel. Even the language in which these crucial experiences are presented varies no more from generation to generation than it does within the career of any one character. Many of the passages so far examined could conceivably have been drawn from the account of any of the three genera-tions—which is only to support Lawrence's claim that in the novel he was less concerned with representing the isolated individual than with discover-ing the generic: each generation is unique in its experience, but on a deeper level it represents in another form "the same single radically unchanged element."

No single metaphor, no single generation, defines the man-woman relation—but collectively they suggest its contours. In each successive cycle Lawrence returns to the same issues, even as he expands his vision to take more and more of contemporary society within his scope. And so in the novel's structure we detect the pattern of repetition coupled with variation, of recur-rence coupled with growth, that we have also found in the language of a brief passage or an entire scene. Lawrence himself, in remarking on the style of Giovanni Verga, described this pattern exactly:

> Now the emotional mind, if we may be allowed to say so, is not logical. It is a psychological fact, that when we are thinking emo-tionally or passionately, thinking and feeling at the same time, we do not think rationally: and therefore, and therefore, and therefore. Instead, the mind makes curious swoops and circles. It touches the point of pain or interest, then sweeps away again in a cycle, coils round and approaches again the point of pain or

interest. There is a curious spiral rhythm, and the mind approaches again and again the point of concern, repeats itself, goes back, destroys the time-sequence entirely, so that time ceases to exist, as the mind stoops to the quarry, then leaves it without striking, soars, hovers, turns, swoops, stoops again, still does not strike, yet is nearer, nearer, reels away again, wheels off into the air, even forgets, quite forgets, yet again turns, bends, circles, slowly, swoops and stoops again until at last there is the closing-in, and the clutch of a decision or a resolve.

This "curious spiral rhythm" is so characteristic of the way Lawrence's mind operates (the style of the passage illustrates the argument) that it can be shown to permeate every layer of his work, from the most local to the most general. Here Lawrence provides a rationale for his repetitions—whether of word, phrase, scene, character or the general movement of a book: he is not engaged in a logical argument, nor is he concerned with exhaustively specifying a milieu or a life; rather he is engaged in refining his own vision of the human condition, in defining what is essential, in identifying the generic.

In the cycles of our moods, in the periods of the physical world, and in our own bodily life, we discover the recursive rhythms of Lawrence's prose. In his foreword to *Women in Love* he himself acknowledged this connection between language and experience:

In point of style, fault is often found with the continual slightly modified repetition. The only answer is that it is natural to the author: and that every natural crisis in emotion or passion or understanding comes from this pulsing, frictional to-and-fro, which works up to culmination.

This defense of his recursive style clearly applies to the many passages in which the imitated rhythm is coital; but it applies equally well to the delicate accounts of day-to-day mutations in love between Tom and Lydia or Will and Anna. The spiral rhythms pursued by the "emotional mind," which Lawrence noted in the style of Verga, inform all levels of his own writing—the syntax of sentences, the pattern of scenes, and the narrative structure of the whole.

"This activity of the mind," he goes on to say in the passage on Verga, "is strictly timeless." Although the generations of Brangwens are temporally related to each other, they are also, like a sequence of metaphors, related atemporally by their common pattern. *The Rainbow,* like *Sons and Lovers* and *Women in Love,* derives much of its persuasiveness from this doubling and trebling of man-woman relationships, each one raising, while revealing different aspects of, very much the same questions. Indeed all the novels recast essentially the same characters, who fight through the same fundamental issues. Lawrence lacked—or at any rate refused to use—the exhaustive moral and social categories employed by Austen or George Eliot. Nor did he often proceed, as Flaubert or James did, by precise linguistic specification of motive and mood. Approximating rather than specifying, as if the experience he represented were not finally compatible with language, he wrote back and forth, character after character, book after book, across very much the same (admittedly ample) terrain, so that the novels collectively read more like a palimpsest than a series of discrete statements.

III. MAN IN NATURE

The characters of *The Rainbow,* like those of Hardy's novels (which Lawrence studied with the painstaking care of an apprentice), are firmly planted in the loam of the earth. Their innermost experiences, their psychic development, their instincts and desires are represented as radically continuous with the forces of generation and the processes of change in the natural world.

The whole of the sheaf-gathering scene in the chapter "Girlhood of Anna Brangwen" could be cited as an incomparable demonstration of this link between psychological and natural rhythms. I quote only a few lines, beginning from the point at which, bearing his load of corn stalks, Will approaches Anna:

> Into the rhythm of his work there came a pulse and a steadied purpose. He stooped, he lifted the weight, he heaved it towards her, setting it as in her, under the moonlit space. And he went back for more. Ever with increasing closeness he lifted the sheaves and swung striding to the centre with them, ever he drove her more nearly to the meeting, ever he did his share, and drew towards her, overtaking her. There was only the moving to and fro in the moonlight, engrossed, the swinging in the silence, that was marked only by the splash of sheaves, and silence, and a splash of sheaves. And ever the splash of his sheaves broke swifter, beating up to hers, and ever the splash of her sheaves recurred monotonously, unchanging, and ever the splash of his sheaves beat nearer.

Here the reiteration of verbal units, the repetition of physical actions and the underlying coital pattern combine to express the mounting emotional tension between the lovers, which culminates a few lines later in a proposal of marriage. In small space, this prefigures the larger rhythms of their married life, the continual recurrence of love and strife between them. Unlike Walter and Gertrude Morel, for whom differences of class and education are basic, Will and Anna seem to fight over issues of sexual and spiritual domination. Although certain social causes for their struggle could be found — Will, like Walter Morel, is frustrated by his work; Anna, like Gertrude Morel, is anxious to make her husband over in her own image — they are not prominent in the novel. In comparison with *Sons and Lovers, The Rainbow* provides little of the data necessary for interpreting the feelings and actions of characters in terms of their social situation. The "natural" conflict, the organic disturbance between men and women in the novel, appears to be rooted so deep in individual character, to be so much a matter of the impersonal unconscious, as to escape social determination.

Consider as a second example the account of Lydia's reawakening, presented retrospectively in the second chapter of the novel. After Lensky's death, and after a period of depression and withdrawal from the world, she is restored to a zest for living and delicately prepared for Tom's courtship by the influence of nature:

> There was a strange insistence of light from the sea, to which she must attend. Primroses glimmered around, many of them, and she stooped to the disturbing influence . . . the light came off the sea, constantly, constantly, without refusal, till it seemed to bear her away, and the noise of the sea created a drowsiness in her, a drowsiness like sleep. Her automatic consciousness gave way a little . . . she found the bluebells around her glowing like a presence. . . . She went past the gorse bushes shrinking from their presence, she stepped into the heather as into a quickening bath . . . one morning there was a light from the yellow jasmine caught her, and after that, morning and evening, the persistent ringing of thrushes from the shrubbery, till her heart, beaten upon, was forced to lift up its voice . . . she would wake in the morning one day and feel her blood running, feel herself lying open like a flower unsheathed in the sun, insistent and potent.

Once again we see a character reacting at first passively, and then willingly, to urging from the natural world. Again the "automatic consciousness" — the false self, social mask, persona, shell — which in Lydia's case has been toughened through suffering, must yield to the unconscious, to the forces of life within her and around her. The phrase "quickening bath" distills the essence of the passage, for Lydia is literally immersed in the "influences" and "presences" of nature. By such terms Lawrence intimates relations that develop unconsciously and involuntarily, between man and woman, or between man and nature.

Lydia's rebirth, a complex and verbally intangible process, is likened to the growth and blossoming of a flower. She emerges from this process sensitive to the urging of a new natural influence, that of Tom Brangwen, "the man who had come nearest to her for her awakening," "the image of power and strong life." The beau, the flowers and the sea manifest the same energy, the same urge, the same quickening. By thus presenting psychological processes in terms of natural ones throughout the novel, Lawrence suggests not just a metaphorical resemblance between the two, but an actual, fundamental connection. According to Lévi-Strauss mythic thought proceeds in exactly the same way, by accommodating human affairs to the patterns of nature—which might account for Lawrence's fascination with anthropological and occult treatments of myth. Through the early three novels culminating in *Sons and Lovers,* he generally followed the dominant nineteenth-century literary tradition of viewing nature from the perspective of man; but in *The Rainbow,* in part due to an increasing disgust with man's works, he came increasingly to view man from the perspective of nature, as one manifestation of the life-process.

This altered perspective is magnificently presented in those justly admired opening pages of the novel. For generations of Brangwen farmers, in daily contact with animals and land and weather, nature has set the terms of existence. Their experience only differs from Lydia's in being continuous:

> They felt the rush of the sap in spring, they knew the wave which cannot halt, but every year throws forward the seed to begetting, and, falling back, leaves the young-born on the earth. They knew the intercourse between heaven and earth, sunshine drawn into the breast and bowels, the rain sucked up in the daytime, nakedness that comes under the wind in autumn, showing the birds' nests no longer worth hiding. Their life and interrelations were such; feeling the pulse and body of the soil, that opened to their furrow for the grain, and became smooth and supple after their ploughing, and clung to their feet with a weight that pulled like desire, lying hard and unresponsive when the crops were to be shorn away.

They furrow the earth like lovers. The intercourse between sun and seed, between men and the fleshly soil, is analogous to the intercourse between man and woman—including the seasons of moods, the cycles of fertility, the periods of gestation and the terms of birth. Thus in Lawrence as in Donne human sexuality miniatures the cosmos.

Like Anthony Schofield, whose offer later in the novel of a purely physical marriage momentarily tempts Ursula, the Brangwen men, immersed in nature, are merely "one with it," whereas Ursula both "saw it, and was one with it. Her seeing separated them infinitely." It is this ability to see beyond the physical, to transcend the fever of procreation, which distinguishes the Brangwen women from the men. The loss of self-control, the yielding to the natural, which Lawrence represents as a brief and necessary interlude in sexual passion, has become a permanent condition of existence for the farmers of the Marsh. Throughout the novel nature remains the matrix of human life, but it is also the source of energies which enables men to transcend nature by constructing and inhabiting a social world. At the opening, the ideal relation between nature and society seems clear: to combine the natural vitality, sensual refinement and warm trust embodied in the life of Tom and Lydia on the Marsh Farm, with the intellectual adventure and communal involvement offered by the greater social world. But by the close of *The Rainbow*, as we shall see shortly, that relation has become extremely problematic. The tribulations of England during 1912–15—a country rent by strikes, fearing revolution, mobilizing for war—lay behind this disillusionment.

Although Lawrence's perception of man as a part of nature is latent in the earlier novels, it only becomes fully manifest in *The Rainbow*. "This is a constant revelation in Hardy's novels," he wrote in that study of the elder novelist, begun in 1914, which revealed more about himself than about Hardy,

> that there exists a great background, vital and vivid, which matters more than the people who move upon it. . . . And this is the quality Hardy shares with the great writers, Shakespeare or Sophocles or Tolstoi, this setting behind the small action of his protagonists the terrific action of unfathomed nature; setting a smaller system of morality, the one grasped and formulated by the human consciousness within the vast, uncomprehended and incomprehensible morality of nature or of life itself, surpassing human consciousness.

This is precisely Ursula's discovery, which encapsulates the view of nature and society in *The Rainbow:*

> This world in which she lived was like a circle lighted by a lamp.
> This lighted area, lit up by man's completest consciousness, she

thought was all the world: that here all was disclosed for ever. Yet all the time, within the darkness she had been aware of points of light, like the eyes of wild beasts, gleaming, penetrating, vanishing. And her soul had acknowledged in a great heave of terror only the outer darkness. This inner circle of light in which she lived and moved, wherein the trains rushed and the factories ground out their machine-produce and the plants and the animals worked by the light of science and knowledge, suddenly it seemed like the area under an arc-lamp, wherein the moths and children played in the security of blinding light, not even knowing there was any darkness, because they stayed in the light.

From his knowledge of Freud and Herbert Spencer, and from his reading of Darwin's *Origin of Species,* T. H. Huxley's *Man's Place in Nature* and Ernst Haeckel's *The Riddle of the Universe,* Lawrence was familiar with the view of man which derived from evolutionary theory—man the biological species, distinguished from other animals only by certain frail and imperfect contrivances such as language, vulnerable to the instincts of lust or aggression which stirred inside him, a scarcely civilized creature capable of surviving only if he acknowledged and reconciled the beast within. Although Zola was certainly influenced by this biological view of man, as Balzac had been by an earlier version, Lawrence may be said to be the first major writer to attempt a thoroughgoing translation of this view into fictional terms. His vision of nature as a living "background" resembles Whitehead's conception of the universe as organism, or Bergson's notion of life as a stream impelled by the *élan vital,* or Teilhard de Chardin's account of the total life-process, all three formulations roughly contemporary with Lawrence's own.

In his novels every passionate encounter between man and woman, every stage in the struggle towards selfhood, every intimate contact with nature leads ultimately into "darkness" or the "unknown." It is as if he forced his characters through the medium of words to the boundaries of language, beyond which they could sense powers and orders of being which neither he nor they could name. This is precisely the dilemma implicit in all writing about God. The theologian can gesture towards the absolute, but cannot reduce it to words. Lawrence's characters—in harmony with Kierkegaard, Tillich and Buber—discover the Godhead within the depths of themselves. It is when he attempts to plumb those depths, when he tries to penetrate the "unfathomed distances" within the self, that his language shows the strain of translating the untranslatable. Dante's God is obscured by an excess of light, Lawrence's by an excess of darkness.

He attributes to his natural order many of the qualities, and much of the language, traditionally ascribed in Judeo-Christian cultures to God. This divinization of the life-process resembles the natural theology which developed in response to Darwin, and which found in the operation of immutable natural laws evidence of a God who comprises the whole of nature. "The universe is a great complex activity of things existing and moving." Lawrence wrote in *Apocalypse*, "and all this is God." His uncannily vital descriptions of nature bear out his pantheistic claim in *The Crown* that "we can only know the *revelation* of God in the physical world."

Nowhere is the essentially religious character of his natural vision more clearly manifest than in *The Rainbow*. Thus Lydia as a mature woman worships the sensual "Mystery"; Anna in her pregnancy dances tribute to her unknown procreative Lord; Will, whose sexual experiences are described in ritualistic terms, preserves his religious passion throughout the trials of his marriage; Ursula translates Christianity into physical terms, desiring Jesus for her lover; and Tom intuits an eternal infinite "greater ordering" in the birth of a child and in the wheel of stars. Many scenes in the novel, including most of those mentioned here, are ritual in the sense defined by Tillich: "symbolic forms in which the religious substance that supports our entire existence is represented in a unique way." Nature for Lawrence is that "religious substance," which is shadowed forth in ritual scenes throughout his works, ranging from the exchange of flowers in *Sons and Lovers* to the brutal human sacrifices of *The Plumed Serpent*. In Christian theology the sacred penetrates the profane; here nature penetrates the human. Biology supplants theology. Fate gives way to natural law.

Thus in Lawrence, as in Rousseau and Wordsworth, nature becomes the divine milieu. J. S. Mill was already complaining in his essay on *Nature* in the 1850s that appeals to a divinized "nature" were being substituted for discredited appeals to God by the followers of that woolly-minded Frenchman Rousseau. Like Freud and Lawrence's influential contemporary T. E. Hulme, Mill mistrusted nature, particularly human nature. Lawrence, on the other hand, like the Romantics before him and like Wilhelm Reich and Herbert Marcuse since, held that man is not inherently corrupt, but is corrupted by his institutions, particularly by those which repress his sexual impulses. For Lawrence this did not mean wholly ignoring Darwin's nature "red in tooth and claw"—after all in *The Rainbow* there are the stampeding horses and the wild beasts wheeling in darkness—but it did mean claiming that men were capable of living much more freely and finely and peacefully than their present society permitted.

His representation of the divine principle as a universal life impulse is consistent with a dominant mode of nineteenth-century thought: Hegel postulated a World Spirit, Carlyle a World Urge, Schopenhauer the will, Bergson the *élan vital* (which Shaw translated into the life-force), Freud and Jung the libido. Meanwhile the physicists were systematically interpreting all natural phenomena as various manifestations of some basic energy. Indeed physics had contributed during that century to the desacralization of nature, what Schiller called the "disenchantment of the world." Along with Ursula's professor at college scientists were asking, "May it not be that life consists in a complexity of physical and chemical activities, of the same order as we already know in science?" For the scientist, if not yet for the general public, nature had lost its mystery. It symbolized nothing, spoke no language.

It is apparent, then, that in *The Rainbow* Lawrence was responding both to the cultural death of God and to the desacralization of nature. When Tom Brangwen gazes at the stars, he sees not only hot gases in motion, but symbols of a "greater ordering." Natural theology served Lawrence as a means of restoring coherence and pattern to human existence—a pattern which he felt Christianity had once provided, but could provide no longer.

> So the children lived the year of Christianity, the epic of the soul of mankind. Year by year the inner, unknown drama went on in them, their hearts were born and came to fullness, suffered on the cross, gave up the ghost, and rose again to unnumbered days, untired, having at least this rhythm of eternity in a ragged, inconsequential life. But it was becoming a mechanical action now, this drama.

The felt need for *some* "rhythm of eternity," for some sense of an underlying pattern, an encompassing process, was a crucial impulse behind Lawrence's work, an impulse which over the last century has become increasingly urgent as our conventional versions of God and our inherited social ideals have lost credibility. I am not suggesting that Lawrence would have agreed with Arnold in viewing poetry or any other literature as surrogate religion; nor that with I. A. Richards he would have hoped for literature to "save us." I am only suggesting that through the novels, above all in *The Rainbow,* he movingly communicated his intuition of a God revealed in the natural order, and in the depths of the self. If one accepts Marx's argument that men in the capitalistic industrial process who are alienated from the products of their labor, are to the same degree alienated from "the sensuous external world," then Lawrence's attempt to reconcile men with nature appears as a necessary step in the reconciliation of men with their own creations. His representation of man as a part of nature should be seen, therefore, not only as one aspect of a larger reorientation of thought about man, which was spurred on by scientific speculation concerning the irreducibly animal component of human nature (a reorientation associated with such pivotal figures as Darwin, Frazer and Freud), but also as a response to the contemporary crisis in religious and social ideology.

The Paradoxical Fall: Eternal Recurrence in *The Rainbow*

Evelyn J. Hinz

Explaining the "essential theme" of his investigation, in his preface to *Cosmos and History*, Mircea Eliade observed: "The chief difference between the man of the archaic and traditional societies and the man of modern societies with their strong imprint of Judaeo-Christianity lies in the fact that the former feels himself indissolubly connected with the Cosmos and the cosmic rhythms, whereas the latter insists that he is connected only with History." No literary work, perhaps, evidences so identical a theme as D. H. Lawrence's *The Rainbow;* for not only does Lawrence contrast the cosmic orientation of man in the past with the historical orientation of modern man — as many modern writers tend to do — but he also directly associates the origins of historical thinking with the Judaeo-Christian tradition. Furthermore, just as archaic man, according to Eliade, regarded a sense of history as symptomatic of his fallen condition — as evidence of his limited point of view rather than as an irreversible curse which would thus be visited upon his descendants — so Lawrence explores the origin and nature of man's fall into history within a context which demonstrates eternal recurrence.

The theme of *The Rainbow* is the Fall from a cosmic to an historical or egocentric point of view and correlatively from a cyclic to a linear and sequential concept of time; but in demonstrating that the historical and egocentric perspectives are limited or fallen ones, Lawrence dramatizes that the cosmic and cyclic *is* the reality. Thus the Fall as Lawrence presents it is not the unique historical occurrence recorded in the Bible; rather the Judaeo-

From *English Studies in Canada* 3, no. 4 (Winter 1977). © 1977 by the Association of Canadian University Teachers of English.

Christian tradition becomes for him the characterizing feature of the fallen world and the force responsible for its historical and ego-oriented character. The Fall he evokes as the prototype for *The Rainbow* is the mythic paradigm behind the Judaeo-Christian redaction, just as the controlling symbol in the work is not the biblical rainbow, but the old natural mythological emblem.

It is at the beginning of *The Rainbow* that Lawrence announces this paradoxical Fall as his theme, but the opening of the novel has been rendered problematic as a result of critical dissension over Lawrence's attitude toward the Brangwen men and women. Hence it will be best to return to the beginning after discovering how Lawrence formulates his governing rationale in other episodes. The "Flood" chapter which appears in the middle of the work and which, as the title of the novel suggests, is thematically central as well, serves perfectly, especially since for some curious reason it is rarely analyzed.

Very drunk, so drunk that he cannot walk "straight," Tom Brangwen leaves the "Angel" inn at eleven o'clock one night. Facing a rainstorm, he takes consolation in the fact that the situation is not new to him: " 'Oh, well,' he said cheerfully, 'it's rained on me before.' " But in addition to personal experience, Brangwen also recognizes a precedent for this deluge, ironically, given the moral of the event, the biblical story of the flood: " 'There'll be no volcanoes after this. Hey, Jack, my beautiful slender feller, which of us is Noah? It seems as though the water works is bursted. Ducks and ayquatic fowl'll be king o' the castle at this rate—dove an' olive branch and all.' " Later, on the road home, the relentlessness of the storm provokes him to comment on the futility of his efforts to improve things: " 'It was a lot of use putting those ten loads of cinders on th' road. They'll be washed to kingdom-come if it doesn't alter.' " Again, however, he finds consolation. First, in the fact that he has a son who has succeeded to the responsibility for such things: " 'Well, it's our Fred's look-out, if they are. He's top-sawyer as far as those things go. I don't see why I should concern myself. They can wash to kingdom-come and back again for what I care.' " Second, he observes that as far as the materials are concerned nothing is ever lost; should the cinders be swept away by the flood, " 'they would be washed back again some day.' " And these two observations lead him to enunciate a general, if drunken, philosophy *de rerum natura:* " 'That's how things are. Th' rain tumbles down just to mount up in the clouds again. So they say. There's no more water on the earth than there was in the year naught. That's the story, my boy, if you understand it. There's no more today than there was a thousand years ago —nor no less either. You can't wear water out. No, my boy; it'll give you the go-by. Try to wear it out, and it takes its hook into vapour, it has its fingers at its nose to you. It turns into cloud and falleth as rain on the just and the unjust.' " By way of conclusion to this otherwise pagan, impersonal, and amoral philosophy, however, he introduces a moral and personal frame of reference: " 'I wonder if I'm the just or unjust' "—at which point, "He started awake as the *trap* lurched deep into a *rut*. And he wakened to the *point* in his *journey*. He had travelled some distance since he was last *conscious*" (emphasis mine).

Lawrence's purpose here is to differentiate between two attitudes toward time, toward man's identity, and toward mythology by way of two respective versions of the "flood." In the pagan version the point of the story—since it has no "moral"—is the absurdity of man's attempt to escape from the natural cycle and the myopia of his belief that it can be altered. Whether he recognizes and appreciates its significance, the rhythm continues. Further, while the rain cycle is a natural one, it is not a motiveless one, not a naturalistic phenomenon, but rather a manifestation of the purposive spirit of the cosmos. Finally, in this version of the flood, security resides in the fact of recurrence and disregard for personality: what is happening has happened before and will happen again, and not in the interests of the individual but in the interests of the continuance of all life in general.

In sharp contrast then is the attitude expressed in the biblical version of the flood. As Ursula, Tom Brangwen's granddaughter, comes to realize— and ridicule—the Noah "myth" purports to be "history," and as such the record of a unique occurrence, with the moral that what has happened will *never* happen again. Her ridicule of the "myth" is an index to the negative and atheistical phase of her development, but it is also Lawrence's way of suggesting what is wrong with the Judaeo-Christian tradition and how it leads to such modern attitudes.

The injunction to multiply and replenish the earth seems to her "merely a vulgar and stock-raising sort of business," while the announcement that " 'the fear of you and the dread of you shall be upon every beast of the earth' " leaves her quite cold, for what is it but "man's stock-breeding lordship over beast and fishes." The Lord's promise that he will never again destroy all flesh by water leads her to wonder, "why 'flesh' in particular? Who was this lord of flesh? And after all, how big was the Flood?" And by way of answering these questions and suggesting that the biblical story indicates a very limited and self-conscious point of view, she imagines how an outsider would relate the episode: "Some nymphs would relate how they had hung on the side of the ark, peeped in, and heard Noah and Shem and Ham and Japeth [sic] sitting in their place under the rain, saying, how they four were the only men on earth now, because the Lord had drowned all the rest, so that they four would have everything to themselves, and be masters of everything, sub-tenants under the great Proprietor." The "rainbow" story in the Bible, then, is a tale of power politics and material greed. The ruling power in this version of the myth is an arbitrary Jehovah who acts in the materialistic and plutocratic interests of a chosen few. Security in this story consists not in the principle of recurrence but just the opposite: the natural symbol of the rainbow has been transformed into an allegorical sign, signifying that this specific historical happening will never be repeated, that there will be no future chaos and by implication no new beginnings.

Associated as aspects of an historical orientation, therefore, are the Judaeo-Christian mentality, a linear concept of time, and social and self-consciousness; associated with a cosmic orientation are a pagan mentality, a cyclic concept of time, and an impersonal sense of identity. To which orientation Lawrence pays allegiance is clear from the negative manner in which he describes Tom Brangwen's "awakening," and his pointed emphasis upon the need to understand the story. It is when Brangwen starts thinking about himself and in moral terms that his "trap lurched deep into a rut" and he begins to think in the historical terms of "the point in his journey." It is when he is not thinking about himself but viewing the situation amorally and impersonally that he recognizes the cyclicality of life: " 'That's the story, my boy, if you understand it.' " The cosmic perspective, then, is the controlling one, the historical is the problem Lawrence is exploring; the former is expressed in the diction and dramatic structure of *The Rainbow,* the latter in the points of view of his characters. Aside from its being essential to an understanding of *The Rainbow,* the importance of recognizing the situation is that one is encouraged to respect *The Rainbow* as a skillful artistic work rather than an undisciplined solipsism, while it also explains why the book poses so many problems for the historically-oriented critic.

A typical "modern" reader, for example, complains that the form of *The Rainbow* is flawed by Lawrence's introduction of characters who have no real significance to the plot of the work: "Tom Brangwen's sons need not have existed for all the difference they make to the story. The younger Tom puts in an appearance to express masculine grief at his father's death . . . and he comes in useful when Winifred Inger has to be gotten out of the way. But a man by any other name . . . would have done as well" (Edward Davis, *Readings in Modern Fiction*). But Brangwen's sons are indeed essential to the plot of *The Rainbow* for it is through them that Lawrence demonstrates that time is not linear and that the death of Tom Brangwen signals not the end of an epoch but rather the beginning of another cycle. Tom Brangwen built the road which the flood washed away; his son Fred will repeat the action; Tom Brangwen dies but Tom Brangwen (the son) lives. At the funeral, Tom reads the nameplate on his father's coffin, a nameplate on which significantly there are no dates: " 'Tom Brangwen, of the Marsh Farm. Born ____ . Died ____ .' "

What the "flood" episode is designed to illustrate is the myopic nature of the historical—including the biblical—perspective. In the biblical version, Noah personally survived the deluge; in *The Rainbow* Tom Brangwen survives impersonally and the principle of continuance is generation. According to the historical perspective, the flood was a unique occurrence; as the title of this chapter and Lawrence's diction indicate, it is a recurring thing: "It happened one springtime when Ursula was about eight years old, he, Tom Brangwen, drove off on a Saturday morning to the market in Nottingham," writes Lawrence at the beginning of the episode, employing the ritualistic "*in illo tempore*" formula and thus suggesting that as a mythic event the flood cannot be restricted to any specific time.

Thus it is that the "Flood" chapter concludes with a different kind of Bible—the "Bible" that Ursula hears from her grandmother and in which the opening tale is explicitly concerned with the historically oriented mentality. This central story focuses upon Ursula's other grandfather, Paul Lensky, a social reformer who, unlike the drunken Tom Brangwen, believed that he was " 'the beginning and the end.' " The moral of that story is the falsity of that idea, for as the grandmother explains, " 'yet all did not depend upon him. Life must go on. . . . We cannot take so much upon ourselves.' " Ursula, we are told, "could not understand" the full significance of such stories, nor does she totally until the ending of *The Rainbow* when, after having herself gone through the experience of thinking that individuality was the goal of life, she realizes "the scope of the vaster power in which she rested." If she does not fully understand at this point, however, she rightly intuits that an historical perspective is a limited point of view and conversely that it is in an impersonal concept of life and an appreciation of the archetypal character of history that security resides. What she senses as a result of her grandmother's stories is "the greater space, the past, which was so big, that all it contained seemed tiny, loves and births and deaths, tiny units and features within a vast horizon," and consequently she concludes "that was a great relief, to know the tiny importance of the individual, within the great past." The anxiety of the modern soul arises from a blindness to one's ancestral prototypes. History and the Judaeo-Christian consciousness place one's fulfillment in the future; according to Lawrence it is in the past that the present finds fulfillment.

Since Ursula's dream of the acorn and kernels at the end of *The Rainbow* is generally agreed to contain the rationale which governs the work, a brief examination of this dream will provide an appropriate conclusion to this general formulation of the theme of *The Rainbow*. The dream, one should notice in the first place, is a delirious one; the perception of the true nature of things, that is, comes to Ursula, as it came to her grandfather, when her *mind* is in abeyance. Secondly, it is a perception that "came" to her; it is not a self-projection or a willed vision but an epiphany, and consequently the perennial question of whether or not the vision is in keeping with her psychological development becomes in one sense irrelevant. A reversal of the Brangwen women's determination to go out and discover the unknown, Ursula's situation is a repetition and fulfillment of the stance of the ancestral Brangwens who "had that air of readiness for what would come to them." Thirdly, the vision comes to her after a ritualistic repudiation of her social and historical identity rendered in terms of first person point of view: " 'I have no father nor mother nor lover, I have no allocated place in the world of things, I do not belong to Beldover nor to Nottingham nor to England nor to this world.' " And finally, what comes to her is the recognition that the life of the kernel, the life of the individual, consists in the creation of "a new knowledge of eternity in the flux of Time." What these key words imply is the necessity to escape not from the past but from the historical concept of the past; for what the dream formulates is the dynamic manner in which the "great past" is repeated in the present.

In each age the eternal manifests itself, but because the manifestation occurs in time, each age gives to the archetype its own signature. Profane history sees only a series of signatures, the "flux of Time." The Bible is merely the signature of the Judaeo-Christian age; it is not the record of the mythic prototypes but rather a record of the way primordial gestures have been played out in a particular culture. The Judaeo-Christian signature, however, consists in the argument that its legends are not archetypal but unique or historical, that the events which it records have occurred and can recur only typologically. Hence the Fall in *The Rainbow* is identified with the adoption of the Judaeo-Christian orientation as symbolized by the "vicar" to whom the Brangwen women turn at the beginning of *The Rainbow* and hence Lawrence's long polemic against Christianity is concerned with the way the mythic concept of periodic regeneration has been replaced by the biblical concept of eschatology, with the way the Judaeo-Christian tradition has straightened the pattern of life.

The role of ritual in a pagan ethos is the abolition of time in the interests of perpetual rebirth; the Christian liturgy emphasizes time and turns the cycle of creation (the whole year) into a broken arc (a half-year): "Alas, that so soon the drama is over; that life is ended at thirty-three; that half the year of the soul is cold and historiless! Alas, that the memory of the passion of

Sorrow and Death and the Grave holds triumph over the pale fact of Resurrection!" The biblical dimension in *The Rainbow* is a negative rather than a positive thing; the Bible is not the thing at odds with the novelistic-historical mode but rather at one with it. The "husk" from which Ursula must break out is her "linear" past; the vision she is granted consists in the cosmic perspective from which her ancestors by way of their Judaeo-Christian heritage have fallen.

The theme of *The Rainbow,* therefore, is what might be called the definitively mythological one—that historical consciousness and its attendant evils are a symptom and consequence of a departure from the paradise of archetypes. History *is* cyclic; life *appears* "ragged, inconsequential" when one is deaf to the "rhythm of eternity" and blind to one's relationship to the "great past." In demonstrating now how this theme is expressed and dramatized in the narrative as a whole, we will discover not only that *The Rainbow* has unity and organic form but that it is a much more structured and literary work than is generally supposed.

That *The Rainbow* has an enclosing cyclic structure must be our first observation since it is here in the broadest manner that Lawrence dramatizes his cosmic perspective. Not only does the work begin and end with the same spirit of expectancy—as there is "a look in the eyes of the Brangwens as if they were expecting something unknown," so Ursula senses something "unexplored" and sees in the colliers "a sort of suspense, a waiting in pain for liberation"—*The Rainbow* also begins and ends in the same place, identified in terms of the church-tower which the ancestral Brangwens see from their fields and Ursula sees from her bedroom. Further it is in the vicarage of this church that Tom Brangwen finds his wife, and it is to a restoration of this church that Will Brangwen devotes his life. In addition to identifying the Judaeo-Christian ethos in which the history of the Brangwens unfolds, then, the church-tower also functions as the mythological *axis mundi*—the fixed centre or world navel from which all creation issues and to which all created things return. To emphasize this mythic symbolic value, Lawrence locates the tower in "Ilkeston," i.e., "same stone," and makes the shutting off of the Marsh from Ilkeston the point at which the history of the Brangwens begins. History begins when one departs from the cosmic centre and its related concept of eternal recurrence.

This observation in turn helps to explain what seems to be a great difference between the beginning and end of *The Rainbow.* Whereas the Brangwens see the church-tower from their fields and see it standing on a hill with "the houses of the little country town climbing assiduously up to it," Ursula sees the church-tower from her bedroom in the town of Beldover, and sees it as an "old church-tower standing up in hideous obsoleteness above the raw new houses on the crest of the hill." What was once a peaceful agrarian setting has become a sordid industrial one. But *The Rainbow* does not end with this contrast, through ironically many critics seem to wish it did. *The Rainbow* ends with Ursula's recognition that all that has changed is the appearance, not the reality. Beneath the "horny covering" is the eternal living spirit. What the surface corruption signifies is merely the end of one cycle—the chaos that eternally precedes the new creation. Hence the critic who argues that "the rainbow which appears at the end of the novel stands not, as most critics think, for the regeneration of society, but for Ursula's new perception," is right in suggesting that Lawrence is not announcing a program of social reform, but he is wrong in restricting the significance of the rainbow to Ursula's new point of view. Her vision is not the "esoteric insight of a single person," but an insight into the true nature of things. The rainbow does stand for regeneration because periodic regeneration is a reality, because as Tom Brangwen said, " 'That's how things are.' " Ursula's perception consists in an intuitive awareness of the cyclicality that Lawrence has dramatized in the structure of *The Rainbow*. What she sees is not a future Utopia but the saga of the Brangwens about to repeat itself once more, the great past about to manifest itself in another present. Her vision of the future is essentially a vision of the past, of the life style of her ancestors; for what the rainbow standing *on earth* signifies is "the intercourse between heaven and earth" that the Brangwen men experience; the "clean, naked bodies . . . rising to the light and the wind and the clean rain of heaven" are the bodies of the Brangwens in their consonance with the cosmos: "sunshine drawn into the breasts and bowels, the rain sucked up in the daytime, nakedness that comes under the wind in autumn, showing the birds' nests no longer worth the hiding." When Ursula perceives of her contemporaries "that the rainbow was arched in their blood," Lawrence evokes the spirit of her ancestors who "knew the wave which cannot halt." As Lawrence's words repeat themselves, so history repeats itself.

" 'How many more Brangwens?' said Tom Brangwen, ashamed of the too-frequent appearance of his family name" during the signing of the register at the marriage of Anna and Will. But not only does the Brangwen name persist as a principle of continuity throughout *The Rainbow*, there is similarly a constant in the names of the foreigners who figure prominently in the experience of each of the respective generations of Brangwens—"-sky" (i.e., Lydia Len*sky,* Anna Len*sky,* Anton Skreben*sky*)—which also defines the symbolic importance of the marriage motif. Furthermore, in addition to their surnames, the first names of the major family members in *The Rainbow* recur, and this repetition from one generation to another constitutes another way in which Lawrence dramatizes the paradox of recurrence in decline.

Alfred Brangwen, with whose marriage the saga proper begins, has four sons. Of the two who play a central role in the narrative, one is named after his father, the other after the ancestral Brangwen, the Tom mentioned in the general opening of *The Rainbow*. Tom Brangwen, son of Alfred, has two sons; to one he gives his own name, to the other the name of his father and brother. Alfred Brangwen, son of Alfred, names his son William; Will marries Anna Theresa and three of their children are named Ursula, Billy, and Theresa, respectively. Though Ursula does not marry, and though she aborts her illegitimate child, she too gives her name to another generation — to the baby daughter of the man who owns the barge, the *Annabel*, after which the baby was originally to be named. As the Alfreds and the Toms suggest, therefore, the names tend to be repeated three times, and thus a pattern of expectation is created which suggests that the baby "Ursula" will also give her name to another generation.

Moreover, in addition to their suggestion of repetition within the history of the Brangwens itself, the names of Lawrence's characters are also designed to make their history a repetition of older and larger historical movements. A frequent observation in interpretations of *The Rainbow* is that "the novel is not only a social history of England, but Lawrence's parable of the history of the human race." Strictly speaking, this is wrong, and the necessity of being precise about the issue is that a misinterpretation of the way Engish and world history function in the work leads to a misinterpretation of the spirit of the work. The critic who makes the above observation, for example, approaches *The Rainbow* as a work designed "to reveal how the modern outlook has evolved" and he describes this evolution as "one of decline." *The Rainbow* does trace the departure from the cosmic centre; it does so, however, not allegorically, but archetypally. The saga of the Brangwens is given a very specific opening date — 1840. The work records, then, only a very modern period of history; if it creates the impression of older and more general movements in history, therefore, it must be because history repeats itself. But if history repeats itself, the pervading spirit of *The Rainbow* is not a sense of what has been "lost" but the sense that nothing is ever lost.

The first individualized Brangwen to appear is the ancestral "Tom" who is introduced by way of the Brangwen women's contrast between their husbands and the vicar. A foil to the type of life represented by the vicar, by way of his Hebraic name Tom also stands in contrast to the non-individualized Brangwen men and their pagan world. Negligible in terms of novelistic plot, then, Tom Brangwen introduces what for Lawrence is the great historical prototype for the departure from a cosmic to an historical orientation—the movement from the pagan to the Judaeo-Christian ethos.

Why the genealogy of the Brangwen race begins with Alfred similarly comes into focus when one recalls his historical prototype, King Alfred the Great, with whom not only the history of England but also the history of England as a Christian nation began. Translator of the histories of Bede into Anglo-Saxon, Alfred the Great also introduced history itself into England. And just as the reign of Alfred was characterized by the Danish invasions, so the "Alfred of this period" in *The Rainbow* witnesses the "invasion" of his land by the forces of industrialism. And just as the economic history of England, and of all nations in general, reflects a movement from simple agrarianism to commerce, so as a result of the advent of industry, the Brangwens "were almost tradesmen." Nor will it hurt, in this context, to notice that the word "trade" originally meant a track or path and a course of regular procedure.

Through the sons of Alfred Brangwen, Lawrence introduces the three great periods that characterize world history as well as British history in particular, and this he does not only through names, but also through situation and allusions. Alfred Brangwen, the oldest of the three sons, recapitulates the Anglo-Saxon heritage of his father at the same time that he "was something of a Prometheus Bound." The second of the trio, Frank, has a Norman name at the same time that he has "features something like a later Roman youth." The youngest son is Tom, who at the age of twelve is sent to the English temple of learning, the Grammar School. As the history of the world, therefore, is a history of the Greek, then the Roman, and then the Judaeo-Christian societies, and the history of Britain consists of the Anglo-Saxon, then the Anglo-Norman, and finally English periods, so in the Brangwen family of the 1840s we have Alfred, Frank, and Tom.

In the marriage relationships and cultural situations of the three generations of Brangwens which *The Rainbow* specifically describes, these great movements are repeated at the same time that their recurrence in later periods of history is suggested. Central to the first generation, for example, is the marriage of Tom and Lydia (a Polish-German woman with a Greek name). The marriage of the Norman Will (William the Conquerer) and the Hebraic Anna (mother of the Virgin Mary) is the focus of the second generation. The relations between the Germanic Ursula (St. Ursula) and the Roman militarist Anton (Mark Antony, the soldier) are the subject of the third generation. Tom Brangwen and his wife live at the Marsh, a simple agrarian life; and though the difference in their language makes verbal communication difficult, they come together in the darkness of sexual intercourse where no articulation is demanded. Will and Anna live in a cottage at Cossethay; a draughtsman in a lace factory, Will is a wood-carver by avocation; a "gallant" and "cavalier" in appearance; the focus of his life is the cathedral and the great art work of the masters. His wife, Anna, is in her puritanical distrust of his passionate response to religion a true daughter of her father Paul (St. Paul) Lensky, an "intellectual." Their marriage consists in a battle for supremacy in which Anna emerges victorious, and then settles down to fulfill the biblical injunction to increase and multiply. Ursula's experiences are located in St. Philip's school in a "poor quarter" in Ilkeston and at the University; it is an age in which the machine has become the god, and God has become remote and Deistic. A liberated woman, by means of her education, Ursula finds no compatible marriage partner; her relationship with the social reformer and imperialist, Anton, is literally and figuratively an abortive affair.

As this survey suggests, the experiences of the three generations of Brangwens reflect in general the cultural and political movements that leads up to the modern period. In the life of Mr. and "Mrs. Tom," in the frequent excursions to the "George Inn" on the part of Tom, in the suggestive toasts which the three brothers drink to the young couple, in the reenactment of St. George and the Dragon at Christmas at the Marsh, we have something of the vitality and earthiness of the Chaucerian and Medieval Age. In Will Brangwen's concern with the great art of the past as well as in Anna's critical temper is suggested the spirit of the Renaissance, while the victory of Anna over Will recalls the Puritan Revolution. In Ursula's development, the emphasis upon learning and the associated skepticism toward accepted beliefs and empiricism with respect to experience evoke the period of the Enlightenment.

The activities and interests of the three generations also can be seen as having been played out in the three phases of the general romantic period leading up to 1840. Brangwen's uncouthness, for example, his homespun philosophy and his dialect, in addition to his interest in the child, Anna, and his ability to communicate with her, coupled with his reaction against learning and yet his love of the sound of poetry are in keeping with the primitivism of the so-called pre-romantic period. Will Brangwen's religious ecstasies and his desire to escape from time, on the one hand, and Anna's delight in nature, on the other, are evocative of the romantic climate proper. In the political and social tone of the chapters dealing with Ursula, and the repeated defeat of her romantic notions by the harsh realities of an industrial world, in the debate with her science instructor over the meaning of life we have the spirit of doubt and disillusionment associated with the age of Carlyle—the last phases of the romantic period.

Finally, Lawrence emphasizes through specific literary allusion that the saga of the Brangwens is a microcosm of the general Victorian period. The two poems that give a distinctive feature to the education of Tom Brangwen are Tennyson's "Ulysses" and Shelley's "Ode to the West Wind," the former a poem about the yearning for an heroic age of adventure and an assertion of will, the latter a hymn to nature which relates social regeneration to its cycles. In view of his passionate concern with art and architecture, one need scarcely have been informed that Will is a devotee of Ruskin. Considering the intense concern of Ursula in particular, but of *The Rainbow* in general, with modern love and the consequences of a Judaeo-Christian orientation, it is similarly fitting that the two works which Ursula receives upon departure from St. Philip's are the poems of Meredith and Swinburne. Why Lawrence chose 1840 as the date whereon to begin the history of the Brangwens and why in addition to reasons already discussed he named his leading Brangwen Thomas now also becomes clear; 1840 was the birthdate of Thomas Hardy, who epitomized for Lawrence the spirit and the problems of the modern world.

A repeated criticism of *The Rainbow* is that Ursula's vision of regeneration is unprepared for and consequently that the work has no proper ending and is unfinished. When one appreciates the way in which Lawrence demonstrates that history repeats itself, however, then the ending of *The Rainbow* appears to be in perfect order. Consequently, for the wrong reasons, those who argue that the work has no ending are right. An ending of the traditional variety would be an endorsement of the historical perspective, the limitations of which it is Lawrence's purpose to dramatize. Appreciating this, furthermore, one best understands the opening of *The Rainbow* and why in one sense neither has the work any proper beginning.

In that "the Brangwens *had lived* for generations on the Marsh farm" (emphasis mine), *The Rainbow* begins *in medias res,* and the purpose of the opening landscape is to characterize the general ethos in which the current generation lives. The main feature of this world is division, and it is first introduced when the setting is given historical location: the Marsh farm is located "where the Erewash twisted sluggishly through the alder trees, separating Derbyshire from Nottinghamshire." Next division is linked with linear measurement and both are associated with a central symbol of Christianity: "Two miles away, a church-tower stood on a hill, the houses of the little country town climbing assiduously up to it." In this context, the tower evokes the legendary "Tower of Babel." And finally, by way of the church-tower the difference between the sky and the earth, above and below, the town and the country, the individual and the group are introduced along with the concept of sequence and cause and effect and memory: "Whenever one of the Brangwens in the fields lifted his head from his work, he saw the church-tower at Ilkeston in the empty sky. So that as he turned again to the horizontal land, he was aware of something standing above and beyond him in the distance." The opening of *The Rainbow* thus presents a divided world and associates this division with history and Christianity.

Immediately following this landscape, however, is a portrait of the generic Brangwen character; and the essential feature of this human landscape is a sense of harmony and security, and an absence of any localizing touches or historical identification. To conclude, as is frequently done, that Lawrence's purpose is to provide an idyllic point of departure for a story of decline, however, is as inadequate as to suggest that his intention is to present a mindless mode of existence from which man must evolve into a conscious mode of being. The inadequacy arises from not attending to Lawrence's explanation of why the Brangwens are presented as they are. The Brangwen race did not always live in accordance with the cosmic cycles; the timeless world they experience at the opening of *The Rainbow* is not the beginning of their history but the beginning of a new cycle. The reason why the new cycle has begun is that "they had *forgotten* what it was to be in *straitened* circumstances" (emphasis mine). Lawrence's point, in short, is that one becomes consonant with the cosmos when one frees oneself from memory and the historical past; moreover, at the same time his purpose is to demonstrate that the new cycle will consist in a repetition of a previous one. The fall from a cyclic to a linear mode that he dramatizes in the general narrative of *The Rainbow* is a repetition of the experience of earlier generations; as the Brangwens' forgetfulness of "straitened" conditions is the origin of their present sense of "surety," so it is Ursula's "forgetting" of the "triumph of horrible, amorphous angles and straight lines" that functions as the prelude to her vision of the rainbow.

For this reason, thematically *The Rainbow* begins with a question to which the entire work may be viewed as an answer: "But heaven and earth was teeming about them and how should this cease?" As a rhetorical device, the question provides its own answer; it is an assertive sentence arguing that things cannot now nor ever will cease; it is a circular statement — how can the cycle of creation cease when the cycle of creation does not cease. As a rhetorical statement the question expresses the cosmic perspective enunciated by the drunken Tom Brangwen and dramatized in both the lifestyle of the Brangwen men and in the structure of *The Rainbow*. Nonetheless the question can also be viewed as an interrogative, and as such it looks backward to the straitened circumstances of the earlier Brangwens and ahead to the chronological development in the narrative of the later Brangwens. The answer to the question, "and how should this cease?" consequently becomes "by adopting a different point of view"—a point of view characterized by a concern with the past and the future and with the difference between the present and these two times. By expressing both these points of view in a single statement, Lawrence provides a miniature of the entire plot of *The Rainbow* and prepares the reader for his version of the fall as presented in the opening description of the difference between the Brangwen men and women.

That there is an Edenic quality to the life of the Brangwen men is frequently mentioned, but there is a strong reluctance to talk about *The Rainbow* in terms of the myth of the fall—when the subject is not introduced simply to suggest the absurdity of such an approach. The antagonism to the possibility stems from the faulty idea that in order to defend Lawrence from the charges of the intellectualists one must make him an advocate of "intelligence, the humane, and the civilized." Were it not that such a mode of defense itself reveals a commitment to intellectual, social, and cultural ideals one could suggest that a better defense could be made by questioning the adequacy of the intellectualist position. As it is, it is best simply to acknowledge the objections.

The reluctance to speak about the fall in *The Rainbow,* on the other hand, originates in the belief that Lawrence characterizes the mode of existence of the Brangwen men as inadequate. The answer to this objection can be made through a careful observance of Lawrence's use of point of view—a procedure which will also suggest the specifically literary significance of the myth for Lawrence and in doing so provide a general justification of the style of *The Rainbow.*

The style in which the Brangwen men are presented is rhythmic, objective, and characterized by an omniscient perspective. The evocation of their lifestyle is structured according to the cycle of the seasons; the description moves from spring to summer to autumn and winter, and the tempo of the men's activities is the tempo of the seasons' energy. Consequently, when we read that "the men sat by the fire and their brains were inert, as their blood flowed heavy with the accumulation of the living day," one must remember that this is a description of the Brangwen men in winter; it is an evocation of their consonance with the time of year, not a comment suggesting habitual sluggishness. The movement from spring to winter, the decline in energy, is an inevitable part of the natural cycle; their dormancy in winter is the metaphoric death that must precede rebirth in spring. The logic of the passage assumes that winter is not the end and that when spring comes they will again feel "the rush of the sap"; for the wave "cannot halt, but every year throws forward the seed to begetting, and, falling back, leaves the young-born on the earth."

This world of the Brangwen men, furthermore, is characterized by the polarity which Lawrence repeatedly announces as the ideal balance; it is a patriarchal world, but not a world without women. The men are active in the spring and summer—the daytime of the year; the women introduced in the autumn and winter—the nighttime of the year. The men are in ascendance in the fields; the women move with "surety" in the house. The men have strength of will and purpose: "They mounted their horses, and held life in the grip of their knees, they harnessed their horses at the wagon, and, with hand on the bridle-rings, drew the heaving of the horses after their will." The "surety" of the women in the house suggests their contentment.

Suddenly the idyll comes to an end; instead of the expected return to spring one reads, "the women were different," and following this observation is the suggestion of the discontentment of the Brangwen women, the inadequacy of the Brangwen men, the opposition rather than the polarity between the sexes, and the reversal of the earlier roles, the women now desiring the life of the "field," the men now content with the hearth. A change, therefore, has taken place; not a change from men to women but a change in *both* men and women—a change from one world symbolized by the Brangwen men to another world symbolized by the Brangwen women. What the change consists in, as Lawrence's style dramatizes, is a change in point of view and its related concept of values which in turn makes for a difference in life style. The world symbolized by the Brangwen men is a unified and cosmically oriented world—*the world* viewed from an omniscient perspective; the world symbolized by the Brangwen women is a divided one; oriented to social, personal, and Judaeo-Christian values and expressed through an individual and historical point of view. In the "men's" world we move through the cycle of the seasons as "they" respond to the rhythms of the cosmos; in the "women's" world we move from "women" to "woman" to "she" to "Mrs. Brangwen" and "the Brangwen wife" as the Brangwen woman expresses her discontentment with her husband, finds him inferior to the intellectual vicar, finds herself and her children "marked below" others in her society and, aspiring to what she believes is a "higher form of being," concludes that the secret of this "finer, more vivid circle of life" is knowledge, education, and experience.

By repeating "she decided"—"She decided it was a question of knowledge"; "It was education and experience, she decided"—Lawrence emphasizes that the "women" section is presented from a specific point of view and consequently that her conclusions should not be assumed as his; while by making her aspirations "beyond herself" a matter of knowledge, he evokes the myth of the fall. Hence just as *The Rainbow* opens with the suggestion of a divided world from which the Brangwen people are redeemed by "forgetting" their "straitened circumstances," so the fall in *The Rainbow* consists in the adoption of an historical point of view accompanied by division.

Accompanying the necessity of recognizing that it is not until after we move into the women's world that the Brangwen men appear inadequate, is the importance of appreciating why the change from the one world to the other takes place — why do the women who move with surety at one point become discontented women at the next? Most misinterpretations of *The Rainbow* arise from a failure to understand that Lawrence provides no *logical* explanation and most misplaced criticism of Lawrence arises from a failure to understand why he does not. Lawrence provides no explanation not because he is "at a loss" to do so, but because the situation is for him a mythic one. And a myth, as he explains elsewhere, "is never an argument, it never has a didactic nor a moral purpose, you can draw no conclusion from it. Myth is an attempt to narrate a whole human experience, of which the purpose is too deep, going too deep in the blood and soul, for mental explanation or description. We *can* expound the myth of Chronos very easily. We can explain it, we can even draw the moral conclusion. But we only look a little silly." To explain the discontent of the Brangwen women as a consequence of the inadequacy of the Brangwen men, or to suggest that the moral of the story is the necessity for civilization are similarly to attempt to draw a conclusion from a work in which the point is simply that this experience is inevitable.

There are in *The Rainbow,* one now realizes, two rainbows: one is the Judaeo-Christian rainbow, the historicized, allegorized rainbow, the rainbow of a self-conscious race, the rainbow which promises a pot of gold at the end; the other is the natural and mythic rainbow, the symbol of eternal recurrence and continual intercourse between the earth and the sky. The purpose of *The Rainbow* is to explore the origin of the chaotic modern world in terms of the process by which the natural symbol became fixed in the sky; but in doing so Lawrence dramatizes that the cycle of creation has not been halted, and thus he evokes the old mythic symbol and its promise. "I do not believe in evolution," he was to write in *Fantasia,* "but in the strangeness and rainbow-change of ever-renewed creative civilizations."

A Long Event of Perpetual Change: The Rainbow

Robert Kiely

Lawrence is not one for anagrams, acrostics, limericks, parodies, or other games with language, but his treatment of marriage in *The Rainbow* is, among other things, an elaborate interweaving of ways of talking about as well as seeing and experiencing the married state. Casting the story as a family chronicle of three generations gives the novel a conventional movement forward. Yet the recurrence of the basic situation—a man and woman attempting to live together—the relative scarcity of historical information, the stability of symbolic language, and the repetition of peculiar linguistic structures counteract the forward motion. In a sense, Lydia, Anna, and Ursula are all contemporaries, as are Tom, Will, and Anton. There is no more finality in the novel than there is in *Ulysses.* Obviously, marriage is not an "end," since, despite the marital achievements of two generations, the book concludes with Ursula Brangwen unmarried, as restless and dissatisfied as her widowed grandmother and foster grandfather were at the novel's beginning.

Lawrence does show the effects of education and the gradual breakdown of rural village life on marriage. Anna's religious skepticism and Ursula's going away from her family to teach and, even more, her taking a lover, are signs of "modern" development. But these external considerations appear, in this novel at least, to interest Lawrence less than the emotional and physical intimacies that change relatively little from generation to generation. In fact, *The Rainbow* can be seen as a family history that, in an odd way, refuses to go forward but repeatedly turns back on itself, as if trying to determine

From *Beyond Egotism.* © 1980 by the President and Fellows of Harvard College. Harvard University Press, 1980.

whether there is a logic in human mating that is stronger than historical circumstances and personality.

Joyce presents the marriage of Leopold and Molly in multiple layers of complex textual variation; Lawrence provides three primary texts on marriage that overlap, resemble, and differ from one another in subtle ways. The first text is essentially that of Tom Brangwen, who does not so much narrate as see and feel what the author records. The second is shared by Anna Lensky and her husband, Will Brangwen, sometimes in dialogue, sometimes by means of a narration with a rapidly alternating viewpoint. The third text is almost exclusively Ursula Brangwen's, with the major exception of a crucial and devastating episode in which the reader is taken into the mind of her lover, Anton Skrebensky. Interspersed among these are commentaries and digressions by minor characters.

Throughout all three marriage narratives, the dominant structural as well as thematic and metaphorical concern is spatial. Marriage is not treated primarily in temporal terms, as a significant moment or an end of significant moments. Rather, it is seen first and last as a matter of place, of a man and a woman coming together to "share a bed," "live under the same roof," and in doing so to create, if possible, a new space. The verbal equivalent of this process is not the exchange of vows—which Lawrence never shows—nor the woman's taking the man's name, but the creation of a new language through which husband and wife not only understand one another but communicate with the world, whether or not the other is present.

Lawrence wastes few words in marrying Tom Brangwen, the young, inarticulate English farmer, to Lydia Lensky, the Polish widow and mother of Anna. On the face of it, there seems to be little to say about them except that they appear to have almost nothing in common, and therefore little to say to one another. When Tom first sees Lydia, he simply thinks to himself, "That's her." When, in fact, he does learn something of her history, he is not really very interested in it: "He had learned a little of her. She was poor, quite alone, and had had a hard time in London, both before and after her husband died. But in Poland she was a lady well-born, a landowner's daughter. All these things were only words to him, the fact of her superior birth, the fact that her husband had been a brilliant doctor, the fact that he himself was her inferior in almost every way of distinction. There was an inner reality, a logic of the soul, which connected her with him."

The facts of this highly concentrated narrative summary are enough for whole chapters in another kind of novel, but Lawrence, through the mind of Tom Brangwen, introduces them only to dismiss them as unimportant to the relationship the two are in the process of forming. It is a curious reversal of the theme and narrative structure of the three short stories discussed earlier, in which the husband's discovery of the wife's narrated text, complete with facts about another life, comes as an overwhelming revelation. Tom finds out about Lydia's other life, her other man, her foreignness and distinctness from himself, at the very beginning. Yet he is conscious of an "inner reality," a "logic of the soul," that does not cancel out these facts but makes room for them. Lydia's difference from himself is not a surprise or a threat. Each feels the awareness of the mystery of the other as a condition of their mutual attraction.

Tom's formal proposal to Lydia is an awkward, impersonal event in which he finds himself nearly speechless and collapses into a chair to recover from faintness. As usual, very little is said. But after Lydia accepts, he leaves the house where she is working and goes into the night, where the activity of his mind—translated into words by Lawrence—becomes indistinguishable from the nonverbal chaos of a turbulent sky. "He could not bear to be near her, and know the utter foreignness between them, know how entirely they were strangers to each other. He went out into the wind. Big holes were blown into the sky, the moonlight blew about. Sometimes a high moon, liquid-brilliant, scudded across a hollow space and took cover under electric, brown-irridescent cloud-edges. Then there was a blot of cloud, and shadow. Then somewhere in the night a radiance again, like a vapour. And all the sky was teeming and tearing along, a vast disorder of flying shapes and darkness and ragged fumes of light and a great brown circling halo, then the terror of a moon running liquid-brilliant into the open for a moment, hurting the eyes before she plunged under cover of cloud again."

The most obvious thing to notice about such a passage in terms of narrative space is its relative length in contrast with the perfunctory summary of Lydia's life in Poland. Even when further details are added to that story in the following chapter, they, like the external details of Lydia's and Tom's day-to-day life together, pale beside the nonfactual, nonlinear, seemingly incoherent efforts to express an inner state of being. In this passage, Tom is responding to the unique and intense experience of the coincidence of "intimacy" and "foreignness," of a union made pleasing to the point of pain by a knowledge of the difference that makes it possible.

The language Lawrence chooses to approximate Tom's state of mind does not refer directly to him or to Lydia, but to the spaciousness of the sky in turmoil. There are intense moments without single direction; great flashes of light without steady illumination; vivid images without apparent pattern or meaning. It is, in other words, the kind of passage in which Lawrence appears to be indulging in Romantic excess and losing control along with his character. In fact, however, the passage has a structure within the "vast disorder of flying shapes and darkness." Words are linked to one another as if in self-defense against the frantic pace of the phrasing. Through hyphenation, internal rhyme, and alliteration, unexpected resemblance and cohesion are revealed within the confusion. Perhaps most important of all is the iteration of the feminine personal pronoun. Early in the paragraph, "he could not bear to be near her" refers to Lydia. In the final clause, the reference is to the moon, fused by grammatical as well as emotional association with the woman whose "radiance" will guide Tom to a new but by no means static sense of place.

Just before the wedding, it worries Tom that "they were such strangers," that "they could not talk to each other." Their conversations after marriage show that, in this regard, there is little change.

> "I'm betimes," he said.
> "Yes," she answered.
>
> "They blow up with a rattle," he said.
> "What?" she asked.
> "The leaves."

Despite its failure to inspire conversation, their union changes both profoundly. Tom does not become more articulate, but his silences result not from a frustrated groping after understanding but from a peaceful rapport with things that resolves the apparent contradiction between detachment and continuity: "It made a great difference to him, marriage. Things became so remote and of so little significance, as he knew the powerful source of his life, his eyes opened on a new universe, and he wondered in thinking of his triviality before. A new, calm relationship showed to him in the things he saw, in the cattle he used, the young wheat as it eddied in a wind."

The elements of external nature are unchanged, but marriage has provided Tom with a key by means of which he reinterprets them, sees them for the first time in relation to one another and to himself that he had not known existed. Once the key is provided, the muddle becomes a language that "shows" itself to him—not an arbitrary invention of his own, but a universal system that was always there, though illegible to him. The remoteness and diminished "significance" refer partly to his past confused view of things but also to the false idea that meaning and importance reside in or behind things in themselves, rather than in relationships. His detachment from this idea and from himself as a "significant" but dead weight is part of his transformation into the wedded state. It, in turn, reveals his unpossessive, living bond with his animals and crops. The symmetrical phrasing, the unhurried pacing, the uncomplicated syntax provide a linguistic contrast to the cluttered and frenzied passage in which Tom watches the moon after proposing to Lydia. They also provide a rhetorical, if not a logical, coherence between two apparently contradictory conceptions, remoteness and binding. At the same time that Tom recognizes that things have become remote after his marriage, he senses a new and calm relationship with nature.

Whatever bond Lawrence is trying to portray through Tom and Lydia, it is not associated with the kind of domestic confinement or coziness so often connected with country marriages. In fact, though Lydia moves into the Marsh, Tom's family house, and they remain there throughout their married life, the inner experience is more like a release from the particularity of place than a restriction to it. The early scenes of Tom at home on the farm are reminiscent of George Eliot's verbal imitation of the Dutch school of painting, all glowing, warm, and comfortable. On one of her first visits to the Marsh before their marriage, Lydia sees the house not at all with the eyes of a Gerty MacDowell eager to move into a dollhouse, but rather with anxious misgivings: "She looked around the room he lived in. It had a close intimacy that fascinated and almost frightened her. The furniture was old and familiar as old people, the whole place seemed so kin to him, as if it partook of his being, that she was uneasy."

The Marsh is for Lydia what Poland and her previous marriage are for Tom, particularly as personified in her child, Anna Lensky. The house, like the child, each with a name that marriage does not change, is an outward sign of an untranslatable past, of an aspect of self that unalterably is. The fact that each partner's difference from the other is so palpable and vivid helps the marriage to avoid the complacency and blindness to distinctiveness that so often comes in unions between people with superficial likenesses of background, class, and nationality — like Gabriel and Gretta Conroy or Gilbert and Angela Clandon.

For Lydia and Tom, the instances of union are extraordinarily moving moments of sharing and transformation throughout their marriage. On the first morning after the wedding, when Anna goes to the bedroom and tries to send Brangwen out of her mother's bed, his answer is a touching expression of his union with Lydia. "'There's room for you as well,' he said. 'It's a big bed enough.'" Later in the year, when Lydia is in labor with their first child, Tom takes Anna to the barn to watch the cattle feeding and, by comforting and cradling her in her distress, makes her his child.

Tom's assumption of the role of father to Anna, like Lydia's moving into the Marsh, are shown, contrary to expectation, as liberating rather than confining actions. Because performed in love and trust—not according to duty or presumption—they become the visible signs of an expanded life in marriage. When, after two years, Tom shows signs of feeling confined, Lydia is able to reveal even further possibilities in their relationship. Though the external contours of this new encounter are emotional and physical, the language used to describe it is again spatial, though with a stronger religious tone than hitherto. "They had passed through the doorway in to the further space, where movement was so big, that it contained bonds and constraints and labours, and still was complete liberty. She was the doorway to him, he to her. . . . He went his way, as before, she went her way, to the rest of the world there seemed no change. But to the two of them, there was the perpetual wonder of the transfiguration. . . . Anna's soul was put at peace between them. . . . Her father and mother now met to the span of the heavens, and she, the child, was free to play in the space, between."

It is important to see that memory, history, and language, like "bonds, constraints and labours," are not so much rejected by this conception of marriage as contained within the vast new space that it creates. The symbol of the arch, which pervades the novel in natural and artificial form, suggests the balance between union and detachment that Lawrence sees as necessary in a true marriage. The bases of the arch remain forever apart while the tops tend inward and join. Marriage is not denied as a social convenience, a meshing of fortunes or families, an orderly means of procreation, a stay against solitude and insecurity, but it is also explored, perhaps for the first time in such depth, as it is experienced by the inarticulate, unhistoric self.

Lawrence, like Joyce, was deeply skeptical of philosophical idealism, yet, also like Joyce, he was drawn to the elements in human character that are universal and unchanging. Lacking Joyce's self-conscious humor, he borrows vocabularies, especially Scriptural, that do not remove his characters altogether from chronology or linear plot, from "bonds, constraints and labours," but reveal them to the reader in a new and unexpected perspective. By the time the passage above occurs in the book, the reader has encountered sufficient instances of the trivial, day-to-day life of the Brangwens to be jolted and refreshed by the language of "transfiguration" and heavenly space. It is as though Lawrence is asking the reader to share vicariously in the rare relationship of Tom and Lydia by following the exhilarating movement of language from the finite to the infinite, to believe in the actual link by traveling the distance he creates between words.

Like Joyce, Lawrence was a novelist's novelist. He loved stories and facts. But, also like Joyce, he was a philosophical novelist who loved ideas and wanted to incorporate them into his fiction. Though it was Joyce who lectured on Defoe and Blake, Lawrence would have appreciated the polarity. Certainly, he shared Joyce's impulse to join the mundane and the mystical in a new narrative form. Their impulses may have been similar, but, little reflects their different backgrounds more than their efforts to wed metaphysics to fiction.

With his "metaphysics in Mecklenberg Street," Joyce is in the great Catholic tradition of Dante, Aquinas, and Chaucer. His interweaving of languages and systems is part of a vast comedy in which learning is elaborately and often beautifully employed to show its own futility and in which form is imposed not because it is a perfect reflection of truth but because, with all its obvious imperfections, it is all that is available to humanity to express what is beyond itself.

Lawrence is closer to the Puritan tradition of Calvin, Milton, and Bunyan, in which learning is used as a weapon to challenge the ambiguities of language and to create ever more perfect forms. If Joyce were to use the word "transfiguration" for an experience within marriage, he would be likely to anticipate the reader's response to linguistic incongruity ironically; his treatment would not necessarily discredit ecstasy but would expose the poverty of language (at least, in the twentieth century) that tries to express it directly. Lawrence, equally aware of the linguistic problem, usually refuses to accept or play with incongruities of this kind. If religious language seems out of place with the sexual character of marriage, the fault is not with language but with conventional attitudes. Perfectly aware when they are "out of place," he flaunts words like "transfiguration," not as sophisticated exposés of verbal inadequacy but as challenges to conscience.

Still, though he does not capitalize on it to the extent that Joyce does, Lawrence is aware of the potential for humor in juxtaposing languages of very different sorts. A mismating of words, as of people, may be a joke as disconcerting and far-reaching in its way as the comic happy matings in the novels of Jane Austen are comforting and significant. When Anna grows up and marries Tom's nephew, Will Brangwen, Tom decides to make a speech at their wedding reception. "For the first time in his life, he must spread himself wordily." Most of the party is drunk while Tom rambles on about marriage, trying to explain and define it: "A married couple makes one Angel." One of his brothers says, "It's the brandy." Another makes a joke about addition. The women begin trading stories about angels appearing in mirrors or getting stuck in noses. Finally, the talk deteriorates into sexual advice to the groom in the form of crude metaphorical banter: "When th' fat's in th' fire, let it frizzle"; "This road can't be lost by a blind man."

Having followed Tom's text this far, the reader may be amused by the colorful language of the wedding guests, but he is more likely to be touched by Tom's awkward attempt to summarize in a speech what marriage means. The image of the angel is neither so foolish as the guests think nor so clear as Tom obviously wishes. The episode adds to our understanding of marriage and the androgynous character of the marital experience, but it adds even more to our comprehension of the writer's difficulty in trying, like his hero, to find the right words to define an experience that is at once public and private, common and unique, physical and spiritual, endlessly discussable and silent.

The discrepancy between Tom's sentimental speech and the crude talk of the guests is laughable, a minor incongruity. But the discrepancy between Tom's earnest analogy and the experience he is trying to describe is of major importance. Tom's "angel," like Lawrence's "rainbow" or "arch," does not "capture" the phenomenon, but one's sense of its failure to do so is a measure of the extent to which the book has convinced us that there is a reality that can only be communicated indirectly. In an imaginative imitation of Tom's rapport with Lydia, the reader can know the author's "meaning" without "understanding" what he says. Between Tom and Lydia and the Angel, between "transfiguration" and "the fat in the fire," are connections that are not altogether frivolous or illogical and still spaces in which to move, interpret, and create for ourselves meanings that Lawrence suggests but does not complete.

The laughter of the wedding guests at Tom's analogy of the angel is an ominous echo of his stepdaughter Anna's laughter at Will Brangwen in church during their first outing together. What initially appears to be the giggling fit of a young girl turns out to be a response as intuitive, inarticulate, and significant as the wordless attraction between Tom and Lydia at their first meeting. Will and Anna share a strong physical attraction, but not long after their wedding it becomes clear that there is an absence of sympathy between them, a discrepancy much wider than mere laughter seems to indicate. The problem is expressed in terms of Will's love of the Church—its music, architecture, and symbolism—which Anna cannot share and, more important, will not let him have as a mysterious portion of himself. Though Anna proves to be the stronger of the two, Will also begins by assuming too much about his wife: "He did not attach any vital importance to his life in the drafting office, or his life among men. That was just merely the margin to the text. The verity was his connexion with Anna and his connexion with the Church, his real being lay in his dark emotional experience of the Infinite, of the Absolute. And the great mysterious, illuminated capitals to the text, were his feelings with the Church."

Will muddles his text by mixing his union with Anna with his attachment to the Church. Unlike Tom Brangwen's deepened experience of marriage as a "transfiguration"—Lawrence's narrated equivalent of Tom's speech about the angel—Will's religious terminology has not been earned through his wedded life. Words like "infinite" and "absolute," so often used by Lawrence in evoking the power of human passion, are almost ludicrously inappropriate to the relationship of Will and Anna because Lawrence will not let the reader forget that they are meaningless to Anna, who "could not get out of the Church the satisfaction he got" but sees everything in concrete, literal, and self-centered terms.

Unlike Tom and Lydia, Will and Anna talk and argue a good deal. They repeatedly disagree not only about the meaning of particular words and images, but about the meaning of meaning itself. Will loves to pore over old books of illuminations and religious paintings. But when Anna looks with him, she cannot share his feelings or let him have them in peace. She becomes furious at the sight of a Pietà:

> "I do think they're loathsome," she cried.
> "What?" he said, surprised, abstracted.
> "Those bodies with slits in them . . ."
> "You see, it means the Sacraments, the Bread," he said . . .
> ". . . It's horrible, you wallowing in your own dead body, and thinking of eating it in the Sacrament."
> "You've to take it for what it means."
> "It means your human body put up to be slit and killed and then worshipped—what else?"
> They lapsed into silence. His soul grew angry and aloof.
> "And I think that Lamb in Church," she said, "is the biggest joke in the parish—" . . .
> "It might be, to those that see nothing in it," he said. "You know it's the symbol of Christ, of His innocence and sacrifice."
> "Whatever it means, it's a *lamb!*" she said. "And I like lambs too much to treat them as if they had to mean something" . . .
> "It's because you don't know anything," he said violently, harshly. "Laugh at what you know, not at what you don't know."
> "What don't I know?"
> "What things mean."

This could almost be a dialogue between a caricature T. S. Eliot, prim and traditional, and a caricature Lawrence, the impetuous and ignorant heretic. In fact, the dramatic context of the dialogue and the complexity with which both characters are presented shows how wrong Eliot was in depicting Lawrence as wild and untutored in comparison with the sophisticated and "orthodox" Joyce. Lawrence's detachment in presenting the argument between Will and Anna is as great as Joyce's is in the famous Christmas dinner debate in *Portrait*. The reader is not invited to side with either Will or Anna, but to perceive, through a verbal confrontation, how the distance between two people can remain barren and unbridged rather than become a fertile space arched over by trust and love.

The chapter is entitled "Anna Victrix," not simply because Anna's will is stronger than her husband's, but because both seem to see the object of marriage, rather like the settlement of an argument, or the editing of a definitive text, as fixed and final. In the debate about symbols and things, one hears Lawrence in both voices, a mind rooted in the concrete, impatient with abstraction, yet continually attracted by the mysterious and infinite potential of things. In certain moods, Lawrence would say with Anna that a lamb is only a lamb; yet in others he knows, with Will, that potent associations carry the creature and the word beyond themselves. As in a marriage, both apparently opposite acts of comprehension need each other. The true visionary must be able, again and again, to humble himself and see the demystified insignificant lamb. Meaning, if it is to exist at all, is what fills the distance between object and subject; it is relationship, and insofar as it occurs between living creatures, it is, by definition, ever-changing.

Lawrence's most extensive exposition of this theme appears in his discussion of law and love in an essay on Thomas Hardy, in which the phrase "artistic form" might well be replaced by "marriage." "Artistic form is a revelation of the two principles of Love and the Law in a state of conflict and yet reconciled: pure motion struggling against and yet reconciled with the Spirit: active force meeting and overcoming and yet not overcoming inertia. It is the conjunction of the two which makes form. And since the two must always meet under fresh conditions, form must always be different." In Lawrence's dialectic, no one can win the argument about the lamb.

The climactic scene between Will and Anna takes place during their visit to Lincoln Cathedral. Will becomes ecstatic over the scope, the symmetry, the depth and darkness of the cathedral, but his idea of space, like his interpretation of the lamb, is utterly different from Anna's. Lawrence's language mocks neither experience. Will's satisfaction with the church is described in terms of sexual consummation: "Then again he gathered himself together, in transit, every jet of him strained and leaped, leaped clear into the darkness above, to the fecundity and the unique mystery, to the touch, the clasp, the consummation, the climax of eternity, the apex of the arch."

The cathedral seems to carry Will away from Anna and she is jealous. What for him is the ultimate is to her, "the ultimate confine," which gives her the "sense of being roofed in." The disagreement here is not over words but, more important for a married couple, over the sense of place. Anna "remembered that the open sky was no blue vault, no dark dome hung with many twinkling lamps, but a space where stars were wheeling in freedom."

The language of Anna's reverie of freedom is as intense and lyrical in its own way as that of Will's communion with the building. Once again, it is not their distinctiveness that ultimately separates them but their inability to love one another enough to accept it. Anna maliciously breaks Will's mood by calling his attention to little carved faces in the stone and insisting that they are of a woman.

> "He knew her, the man who carved her," said Anna.
> "I'm sure she was his wife" . . .
> "It's a man's face, no woman's at all—a monk's—clean shaven," he said. . . .
> "You hate to think he put his wife in your cathedral, don't you?" she mocked, with a tinkle of profane laughter.
> And she laughed with malicious triumph.

What began as girlish giggling at her young man in church turns into a wife's mockery. Anna's laughter and Will's petulance are gestures of repudiation and refusal, not of ignorance or incomprehension. It is because she knows what he is experiencing in the cathedral without wanting to share or allow it that her interruption is so well calculated to destroy his pleasure. From the beginning, Will and Anna know much more about one another than Tom and Lydia, and they talk a great deal more. But their knowledge and words have no power whatever to soften their wills or bring them together. What Tom calls "the logic of the soul" is missing. Their conversations are no improvement on the silences of Tom and Lydia; even their arguments are not exchanges of ideas so much as statements of fixed positions. The debate over whether the carved head is a man or a woman is their perverse and articulate variation on Tom's halting description at their wedding feast of an angel as "the soul of a man and woman in one."

Will and Anna stay together; their physical passion even increases, but their souls remain separate and their discourse hollow. In a summary of Will's defeat, Lawrence observes that "he had failed to become really articulate, failed to find real expression." Thus the collapse of his marriage is seen to result in a failure of language, understood in the broadest sense as the means by which a person establishes relationship between the self and the world.

Unlike Tom, Will sees no "calm relationship" in things. His carvings remain incomplete, his drafting becomes mechanical, his talk with his wife is reduced to faltering quarrels, even his bond with Ursula, the daughter who most loves him, is blighted.

Ursula Brangwen is damaged by the incompleteness of her parents' marriage. Her lack of confidence in herself and her ambivalent feelings about love, though "modern" in expression, are treated by Lawrence as a curse visited on the child because of the sins of the parents. In one episode Ursula and her lover are strolling by a river and talking. Their talk is even more argumentative than Will's and Anna's. It is also more repetitious, almost ritualistic in its rigid stylization. It is talk so filled with irony that definitions are disputed as a matter of course. A word uttered by one partner is repeated by the other in an utterly different tone and tossed back. The effect of the repetitions is the reverse of that of the euphonic word linkings in the night passage following Tom's proposal to Lydia, in which subtle, unexpected harmonies are discovered to exist in the midst of apparent chaos. With Ursula and Skrebensky, the surface order of two lovers walking arm in arm, engaged in seemingly calm and rational discourse, is in fact a chaos of noncommunication, the prevention of meaning.

An extraordinary parody of a human exchange ends in the repetition of the word "nothing," which sums up its meaning: " 'It seems to me,' she answered, 'as if you weren't anybody. . . . You seem like nothing to me.' " Each speaker negates the other by using language as a hard surface. For Skrebensky it is a protective shield; for Ursula, a mirror of ridicule with which she tries to expose her lover's folly and conceal herself. The tone of the dialogue makes it seem part of a dead ceremony, and, in fact, it follows the celebration of a family wedding. Ursula is dressed in white, and bits of confetti are still in her hair. As the two walk away from the family party to stroll along the river, they appear to be rehearsing for their own wedding, but the rehearsal, like the exchange of words, is the sharp antithesis of communion.

The only genuine exchange occurs when Ursula boards a dirty river barge and offers her name to the infant daughter of the bargeman and his wife. The couple have been quarreling and are delighted with the beautiful lady's exotic name. They accept the offer, and Ursula gives the child her necklace as a token of the occasion. The bargeman watches Ursula, who is radiant and "white as a moth," "as if she were a strange being, as if she lit up his face." Once again, the image of an angel suggests itself. Ursula has appeared like a guardian angel to these poor and grimy people, given their daughter a mysterious name with a precious token, and disappeared with a smile.

The scene has a kind of charm, largely because of the spontaneous warmth and gratitude of the couple, especially the husband. But on Ursula's side, it rings false. Her "angelic" gesture is a whim to spite Skrebensky as much as to indulge her own sentimentality. Ursula appears to be acting out an unconscious wish for marriage without a husband and childbirth without a father. Giving away her name and necklace to the infant simply adds a spurious baptism to a false marriage. To call the strangers' child Ursula is another form of repetition, an extension of the conversation with Skrebensky, in which the self is asserted and reasserted with reference to no one with whom a relationship can be formed. There is no doubt that for Ursula the key to the infant's appeal is the fact that she will never see her again.

Given the scenes in the Marsh between Tom and Lydia and in Lincoln Cathedral between Anna and Will, the treatment of space in the section that focuses on Ursula and Skrebensky is telling. One of Ursula's pronouncements while walking with Skrebensky is, "I hate houses that never go away, and people just living in the houses." It seems an idle and passing remark until later, when it becomes clear that Lawrence is going to carry the logic of this kind of talk, as well as the complementary structures of his narrative, to an extreme conclusion. At first the reader takes it as a sign of Ursula's "advanced" ideas as well as a "sign of the times" that she and Skrebensky made love before discussing marriage. But soon it becomes clear that Ursula's preference for love in the woods is not a wholesome sign of liberation, but a hysterical attempt to dissociate love from society so completely that it is not merely marriage, home, and family she is fleeing but the presence of any company at all, including that of a lover.

Acts of individual rebellion can appear as remote from life as automatic collective rituals. If law without love is rigid and sterile, love without law is the chaotic lurching of will running wild. A reader who, with Joyce, thinks of Lawrence as continually defending "nudity in the woods" may be surprised by his ability to show it as a laughable, almost insane form of a childish and willful autoeroticism. While they are guests in the country, Ursula is forever leading Skrebensky on long night excursions on the downs. "Skrebensky wandered dazed, not knowing where he was or what he was doing with her. . . . She would not love him in a house any more. She said she hated houses, and particularly she hated beds."

Lawrence goes on to describe a midsummer evening that for other pairs of his lovers might be a perfect and glamorous setting. But for Ursula and Skrebensky the mood is strange, forlorn, obsessive. "She took off her clothes, and made him take off all his, and they ran over the smooth, moonless turf. . . . And then suddenly she started back, running swiftly. He was there, beside her, but only on sufferance. He was a screen for her fears. He served her. She took him, she clasped him, clenched him close, but her eyes were open looking at the stars, it was as if the stars were lying with her and entering the unfathomable darkness of her womb. . . . It was not him."

Ursula's space, far from being shared with Skrebensky as Tom's and Lydia's was shared, is gained at his expense. The more she expands, the more he contracts, until he is "clasped" and "clenched" into something that occupies no space. He becomes what she has called him from the start, nothing, "not him." He is, for her, a soulless accomplice in her "intercourse" with the stars, which is really to say that he is an accomplice to her illusion, since the unspoken but right word for her act is masturbation. She is not entering the night, but rather imagining that it is entering her through his body. The sexual drama could hardly be more different from the comparatively innocent outdoor love scenes in *Lady Chatterley's Lover* or *Women in Love*. Indeed, it might be more accurate to say that there is no sexual drama at all, but merely an erotic monologue.

The final love-making scene between Ursula and Skrebensky takes place on a beach. It is one of the few episodes in which the narration takes Skrebensky's feelings into account. Through much of Ursula's text, he is depicted as a forerunner of Gerald Crich, attractive and virile, but a kind of hollow machine that behaves and speaks automatically. Ursula's frustrated petulance and even her narcissicism seem understandable, given this view of Skrebensky. But when she refuses to marry him and he breaks down and weeps, the reader, if not Ursula, begins to see him as something other than a tin soldier. The coming together on the beach is a test he is destined to fail. It is described primarily as he experiences it; Ursula's hunger for freedom and space are translated into confinement, suffocation, and death for him. "She seized hold of his arm, held him fast, as if captive, and walked him a little way by the edge of the dazzling, dazing water . . . she clinched hold of him . . . she fastened her arms around him and tightened him in her grip. . . . He knew what she wanted. . . . He felt as if the ordeal of proof was upon him. . . . He came direct to her, without preliminaries. She held him pinned down at the chest . . . it was agony to his soul . . . he wanted to be buried. . . . He felt as if the knife were being pushed into his already dead body."

Ursula, too, seems dead, her "rigid face like metal in the moonlight," her eyes "fixed" and "unseeing." Skrebensky wanders away from her along the beach and finally curls "in the deepest darkness he could find, under the sea-grass, and lay there without consciousness." The confinements of bed, house, and marriage have been avoided, leaving two experienced bodies with virgin souls dead on the strand.

As in the short stories about marriage in which the wife's narration is ignored until a moment of crisis, this is a case of catastrophically uninter-polated texts. The reader is presented primarily with Ursula's version of things and, only when it is too late, is forced to see that Skrebensky might have told the story differently. But it does not really matter. Each wished to impose will and words on the other. It is as though an author, through a trick of rhetorical coercion, tried to be his own reader in order to ensure that his writing would be interpreted only *his* way. Lawrence, despite his own overac-tive will, saw the calamitous futility of such an ambition. He saw that it was the surest way to kill a book as well as a marriage. The "resemblance is not fortuitous," as Frank Kermode has observed. "A novel might resem-ble a Lawrentian marriage . . . since they are both types of the living universe."

Anna wanted to turn everything into nature, to demythologize the lamb. Her daughter wants only spirit. But after much suffering and disappoint-ment, the sky-entranced Ursula realizes that "the rainbow stood on the earth." For Lawrence, the angel, the lamb, and the Gothic arch lose vitality and mystery if bound too rigidly to the earth, but they become impotent and lifeless if allowed to float detached in the ether. Space is a given in creation, yet the recognition and filling of it, the mediation between poles, is an essential act of human comprehension, a reverential engagement in life that imitates what Saint Paul refers to as Christ's saving act of "reconciling in himself the heights and the depths." The mating of man and woman has a potentially sacramental, even divine, meaning for Lawrence, since for him, as for Tom Brangwen, it is not within the power of man or woman to enact the recon-ciliation alone.

Like the silences and gaps between words, space can either separate or unite people. After their final embrace on the beach, Skrebensky literally drags himself away from Ursula and wanders down to the water's edge. At the novel's end, he is in India and she in England. His telegram, "I am married," uses words to express the social as well as the spiritual and geographical distance between them. In the most important sense, they have never really touched one another. Their physical separation at the end is simply the dramatic embodiment of the emptiness that has always existed. In the end, they are "finished" with one another because all along they have both been fixed and finished characters with no capacity to bend or grow.

Their situation provides a striking contrast with that of Ursula's grand-parents. As Tom Brangwen tries to prepare himself for Anna's wedding, he is startled to realize how "unsure," "unfixed," "unfinished," "unformed," he feels as a married man of forty-five. But as Lawrence has him realize, that is precisely the clue to his success as a man and husband. "He might be getting married over again — he and his wife. He felt himself tiny, a little, upright figure on a plain circled round with the immense, roaring sky: he and his wife, two little, upright figures walking across this plain, whilst the heavens shimmered and roared about them. When did one come to an end? In which direction was it finished? There was no end, no finish, only this roaring vast space. Did one never get old, never die? That was the clue. He exulted strangely, with torture. He would go on with his wife, he and she like two children camping on the plains."

Not only does Tom continually relive his own uncertain betrothal, but his words call the reader back to the legendary beginnings of the human race. The echo of the last lines of *Paradise Lost* is unmistakable:

> In either hand the hastening angel caught
> Our lingering parents, and to th' eastern gate
> Led them direct, and down the cliff as fast
> To the subjected plain; then disappeared.
> They, looking back, all the' eastern side beheld
> Of Paradise, so late their happy seat,
> Waved over by that flaming brand; the gate
> With dreadful faces thronged and fiery arms.
> Some natural tears they dropped, but wiped them soon;
> The world was all before them, where to choose
> Their place of rest, and Providence their guide.
> They, hand in hand, with wandering steps and slow,
> Through Eden took their solitary way.

The Miltonic picture of man and woman, abandoned together on a vast plain, as Matthew Arnold recalled, is one of danger and desolation. But it is one of enormous scope and promise as well, the end of one story but the beginning of innumerable others. The archetypal husband and wife are vulnerable, interdependent, more like children than gods. Their union is hardly a sign of the triumph of the individual will, a finished life, or a conclusive plot. Rather, it is the opposite: a reminder of limitation, of the insufficiency of self, the uncertainty of the future and of the earth waiting like a great blank page to be written on by "wandering steps and slow."

The Three Angels in *The Rainbow*

Daniel J. Schneider

> *No, no, it is the three strange angels.*
> *Admit them, admit them.*
> —"Song of the Man Who
> Has Come Through"

Lawrence was never a timid artist, and when he began *The Wedding Ring,* which became *The Rainbow* and *Women in Love,* his daring was immense. His well known letter of June 5, 1914, to Edward Garnett about Marinetti and the futurists; his excited talk about the soul's "allotropic states" and the *"non-human* quality of life" (letter of September 21, 1914); his concomitant interest, as he wrote "Study of Thomas Hardy," in a theory of history and in "the vast, unexplored morality of life itself"; his conviction, as he revised the novel, that "it's great—so new, so really a stratum deeper than I think anybody has ever gone, in a novel" (letter of March 11, 1913)—all this testifies to his conviction that he had "come through" in his efforts to construct an "answer to the *want* of today: to the real, deep want of the English people, not to just what they fancy they want" (letter of February 1, 1913). A new psychology and a new religion were to be blended in his vision of life; and he had found the technical means by which the blending might be effected. He had developed a vocabulary to define the nature of the unconscious motive forces within the psyche, as well as the laws governing their action. He had discovered, too, a form that would present the moral and religious journey of mankind in its quest for fulfillment, a form that would telescope, over three generations, the development of life from tribal unconsciousness to civilized consciousness and that would exhibit the difficulties at every stage

---

From *D. H. Lawrence: The Artist as Psychologist.* © 1984 by the University Press of Kansas.

113

of balancing the desire for independence and the desire for connection with others. The progress of the generations would be, moreover, a recapitulation of the progress of the individual: the ontogeny would recapitulate the phylogeny, and the record of mankind's growth—from childhood to adolescence to a dubious maturity—would be the record of each individual's moral and psychic experience. It is hardly surprising that Lawrence, seeing suddenly the beauty of his new project, was exhilarated. Scientific naturalism, religion, morality, history, sociology—all would be gathered up in this new novel; the method would be, as he said, "exhaustive" (letter of January 29, 1914). If he could only be "sensitive, subtle, oh, delicate," "a fine, an exquisite chisel," he might "find the Hesperides." I imagine him, in writing the novel, as opening the door, with passionate expectancy, to "the three strange angels"—let us call them the angels of religion, of science, and of mimetic art. But in admitting the three angels into his novel, he again posed difficult problems. For each angel had a different message to deliver, and the task Lawrence set for himself was to find a way to blend and harmonize the three voices. That blending, I think, is almost wholly successful. Critics are dissatisfied with the forcing of the ending, with the lapses of "psychological realism," or with Lawrence's preaching—his drawing upon resources "alien to the book," thus becoming a "propagandist" in the later part of the novel. But much of the criticism issues from a failure to appreciate the uniqueness of the form Lawrence created. Before defining the nature of that form, I must examine the separate tasks of the three angels.

THE ANGEL OF RELIGION

The angel of religion seeks to convert the novel into a quest for the rainbow. This angel requires that all of experience, all of history, be viewed as a moral journey toward "maximum of being," from the dark to the light, from the Father to the Son, and then toward the reconciliation of the Holy Ghost—a journey toward the apocalyptic new heaven and new earth. On this journey the pilgrims of the apocalypse encounter the demons and dragons that the devil of "halfness" puts in the way. The novel becomes a *Pilgrim's Progress,* enacting, as Frank Kermode and Mark Kinkead-Weekes point out, the ages of Law and of Love, dramatizing the dangers and the temptations that threaten the sincere seeker, and holding out the promise of salvation in the rainbow.

Every stage of the journey is evaluated in relation to the moral evolution of mankind. The Old Testament world of the Father (i.e., of Tom Brangwen), of the undifferentiated tribal mass, which passively accepts the Law and the fixed form of sensual life, provides a fulfillment of sensual desire; but Tom remains inert, incapable of journeying into the beyond, into the light of the spirit. The world of the Church also proves to be incomplete; fulfillment through blind faith in the creative mystery becomes impossible when skepticism and rationalism erode the Catholic solidarity. As for the modern world, in which mind and spirit (the Son) dominate, it too fails to achieve "maximum of being." Living only from the "upper centers," especially from the spiritual will, modern men and women create a world whose form is as fixed and static and limited as that of the ancient world. True balance and fulfillment is impossible in such a world; indeed, the denial of the blood drives men into perversity, sensationalism, and reduction—the madness of systematic bullying and ego competition. At the end of *The Rainbow* there remains only Ursula's vision of a new heaven and a new earth; but the world is the devil's, and mankind has, up to this point, failed in its quest.

As a religious allegorist, Lawrence, like Bunyan or Spenser, seeks to define both the evils confronted by mankind and the true path to salvation. Thus Lawrence is driven to create quasi-symbolic characters who would corrupt the true believer. These villains, whom Lawrence condemns sharply, are Miss Inger, Uncle Tom, and, to a lesser extent, Anton Skrebensky, all of whom represent the hideous domination of the spiritual will and the ugly failure to heed the promptings of the Holy Ghost. Miss Inger, perverse and willful, seeking only her own triumph, is a Duessa who would lead Ursula into the abyss of cold sensationalism and into the deeper abyss of machine- and Moloch-worship. For the sake of power, Uncle Tom, a nihilist and a cynic, accepts the machine and all the degradations that issue from the worship of the Lord of the Flies. Anton Skrebensky, the army engineer who serves the state and materialism, is a modern nullity, inert and undeveloped. Confronting these three representatives of the modern Age of Love, Ursula learns that the way of the spiritual will is a dead end. The angel of religion summons Ursula to search for one of the Sons of God, who worship the lord of the two ways, of darkness and of light. But Ursula will not meet one of the Sons of God until later, in Birkin of *Women in Love.*

The condemnation of the Age of Love is explicit and severe: Miss Inger, Uncle Tom, and Skrebensky anticipate the vile Loerke of *Women in Love,* who reduces life to pure mechanism, pure utility, pure willfulness; Lawrence approaches, in parts of *The Rainbow,* the bitterness and horror that inform the whole of that *Dies Irae* published in 1920. But Lawrence's moral judgments extend also to the Age of Law, in which men live in the drowse of the blood intimacy, in passive or "female" submission to the tribe, the undifferentiated mass. Tom Brangwen, challenged by a new world of subtle intellection, drinks himself into unconsciousness and burns out his soul. He fails to discover a meaningful life or meaningful work. All of his creative, purposive desires remain frustrated; so he dies in the dark waters of the unconscious, the waters from which he has never been able to emerge. Lydia, too, remains unfulfilled in her soul: the man she yearns for would combine the sensuality of Tom and the intellectuality of her former husband, the Polish doctor and patriot.

In the second generation, Anna gives up her journey into the unknown and lapses into a continuous rapture of motherhood, like one of the fat cabbages that Lawrence condemns in "The Crown." Will Brangwen remains undeveloped and molelike until the extremes of perverse sensation seeking bring about "a passion of death." The plunge into sensation satisfies his craving for a sensual absolute, and he is partially liberated and enabled to turn to purposive work in the world of light. But Will, unlike Birkin, never challenges the form of modern life. Will's entrance into public life—teaching woodworking in Cossethay—is positive; but he never learns that the good man is a fighter, one who fights to break the old form of life.

All of the characters therefore fail in their quest, and all are judged. Even Ursula is condemned at one point. Indeed, she condemns herself for her perverse desire to triumph over Skrebensky and for her destructive spiritual willfulness. The novel may be regarded as wholly formed by the angel of religion and as the inevitable product of Lawrence's conviction that "the essential function of art is moral"; the function of the novel is to lead "into new places the flow of our sympathetic consciousness" and to lead "our sympathy away in recoil from things gone dead."

The Angel of Science

Even readers like Leavis, however, who would stress the moral function of the art, recognize that much of the time Lawrence's characters are creatures driven by irresistible desires and compelled to act as they do: they are amoral, beyond good and evil. Most of the characters are seen, in the manner of Emile Zola or George Moore, in almost purely naturalistic terms. We are asked to view the characters' behavior from the perspective of the Angel of Science, Lawrence's "subjective science," which was deduced, as he tells us in *Fantasia,* from the novels and poems, from "pure passionate experience."

His scientific induction is strongly at work in *The Rainbow:* Lawrence is making a concerted effort to formulate the laws of psychic conflict, to determine the ways in which conflicting motive forces are manifested in normal human interaction. In scene after scene, we find more or less invariant patterns of psychic interaction in the allotropic behavior of particular people. Tom Brangwen, Will, and Skrebensky are all different; yet in their relationships with women they repeat the same patterns of psychic interaction. The same motivations and the same causes of failure are traced. So carefully are these patterns exhibited that *The Rainbow* might be taken as a primer of psychology, a psychology that postulates the desire to "come into being" as the deepest motive and that traces the action of this motive in the opposed love and power urges, both sensual and spiritual. The forms of psychic interaction are laid bare in three great phases of the individual's life: in courtship, in marriage or sexual love, and in subsequent efforts to transcend the limitations of love.

Courtship: The Impulse toward Unison versus the Impulse toward Individuation. In chapters 1 through 3 we saw that two great primal desires originate in man's nature. The first of these is the desire for unison or oneness with the infinite from which man derives, a desire manifested in man's relationship to woman, to humanity, and to the cosmos, or to "God." The self, split off from the whole, wants the joyous enlargement of self that occurs in the love relationship. The deep craving for union with the All is present not only in personal relationships but also in man's desire to "be unanimous with the whole of purposive mankind." This desire becomes man's "societal instinct," his "ultimate need and desire" to work with other men to "build a world . . . something wonderful." As Lawrence said in a letter to Bertrand Russell on July 15, 1915, "The *most fundamental* passion in man [is] for Wholeness of Movement, Unanimity of Purpose, Oneness in Construction." Finally, that desire for "assimilatory unison" becomes a "God-passion," a desire for a "pure relationship" with the entire living cosmos, a desire to connect "religiously" with the inhuman world whose vibrations flow into man and are inseparable from his being.

Yet in seeking maximum of being in the All, the psyche fears that it will lose its own identity. Recoiling from sympathetic union, the psyche asserts, "I am I, I am not these others." A voluntary center is born, the center of assertive individualism. Herein lies the dilemma for the soul. The desire to remain separate and free conflicts with the desire to merge with the Other, to the point of self-obliteration.

Now it is impossible for the individual to remain isolated from the Whole. The isolated self is afflicted by a sense of insufficiency, meaninglessness, or emptiness. The psyche recognizes that it is "derivative," incomplete, or part of a greater reality. Hence the desire to connect with other beings or with Being itself cannot be denied. "Without God we are nothing." In the earliest stages of a relationship, the male seeks completion in woman, and she is identified as his gateway to the Absolute.

So Tom Brangwen, in the first generation, knowing that he is "only fragmentary, something incomplete and subject," and fearing that he must "remain as a nothingness" unless he connects with the "greater ordering," turns to Lydia Lensky, feeling that "with her, he would be real. . . . she would bring him completeness and perfection." So much does she mean to him that he feels "reverence and fear of the unknown," which change "the nature of his desire into a sort of worship"; he wants to "give her all his love, all his passion, all his essential energy." For she is "the symbol of that further life which comprised religion and love and morality," the "embodiment of all the inarticulate, powerful religious impulse."

At first "a daze had come over his mind, he had another centre of consciousness," and he submits to "that which was happening to him, letting go his will, suffering the loss of himself." But this sympathetic impulse toward unison conflicts with his fear of losing himself. Afraid, he wishes "to escape her," and he feels a "fury . . . destructive," an impulse of "revolt" from her attraction. She, too, though stirred by "a quick, out-running impulse" and wanting "this new life from him," feels that "she must defend herself against it, for it was a destruction": her independence is threatened. When Tom proposes, the scene becomes a series of attractions and withdrawals, a to-and-fro of sympathetic and voluntary impulses. He asks her to marry him, and she quivers, "feeling herself created, will-less, lapsing into him, into a common will with him." She "flows" toward him, her eyes "newly-opened"; but it is "sheer bleached agony to him, to break away from himself." Presently he succumbs to "the fecund darkness," a "womb of darkness" in which he is "newly created." A few moments later, however, he feels "a certain negation of him" in her "tiredness," and she seems "to ignore him." He tries to make her his, but he is "afraid," and Lawrence observes, "again he had not got her." She turns away; then she returns to him and responds with passion. Then, because her passion comes "thundering at him till he could bear no more," "he drew away, white, unbreathing." Shortly thereafter, "she was drifting away from him again," but she agrees to marry him, and the scene ends with his contemplating the moon — the female — running into the open, then plunging under cover of a cloud.

The structure of the flashback in chapter 2 is similar. Lydia, who lives in darkness and abstraction after the death of her first husband, is awakened by the light, the positive male creative force. The light rouses her to attention, but then she shrinks away again, "back into her darkness." The morning, the light, beats in on her again until she, "resistant, . . . knew she was beaten, and from fear of darkness turned to fear of light." She wants to be safe in "the old obliviousness, the cold darkness," and she "lapses into" her old isolation with "a will in her to save herself from living any more." But the sun beats in, and she begins to open up. Again, she lapses into "stupor and indifference"; again she opens and becomes "receptive to him"; then she closes "again, away from him, was sheathed over, impervious to him, oblivious"; but again she begins "to open towards him." The oscillations proceed until she agrees at last to marry him.

In the second and third generation these oscillations are repeated, though with a significant difference. Sympathetic union is more difficult in the second generation. Yet Will, like Tom, is filled with a joyful sense of completion when he turns to the female. When Anna tells him " 'I love you, Will, I love you,' " he feels suddenly that "the veils had ripped and issued him naked into the endless space. . . . Whither, through this darkness of infinite space, was he walking blindly?" Anna's "bright, transfigured face" is associated for him with "the Hidden Almighty"; she becomes "the essence of life." And he, "ridden by the awful sense of his own limitation," feeling "uncompleted, as yet uncreated," "wanted her to come and liberate him into the whole." Note that the cathedral in which he worships the absolute, the infinite, is female.

But in the remarkable sheaves-gathering scene, the sympathetic impulse conflicts with the voluntary urge to be separate, free, "unmixed" with another person. At the beginning of the scene, Lawrence tells us that Will and Anna were "separate, single"; but as they gather the sheaves, each working a separate row, they draw together: Will approaches Anna; then "she turned away toward the [female] moon"; then she returns again ("She was always first," Lawrence notes); but when Will again approaches, "she turned away." Again, she "walked toward him"; then "she broke away, and turned to the moon"; then, "he was drawing near, and she must turn again." The oscillations proceed—a "moving to and fro in the moonlight"—until at length Will overtakes her and kisses her, whereupon he feels "possessed" of the "night" and trembles "with keen triumph."

The sheaves-gathering scene presents a seesaw, a contest of wills: "His will drummed persistently, darkly, it drowned everything else"; and the moonlight to which Anna turns is symbolic of the virginal female, intact, complete, and separate. The contest of wills is a struggle for "triumph," and it ends with Anna's victory over Will: "He was hers. And he was very glad and afraid." Once he commits himself utterly to her, however, she draws "away from his breast," rather like the heroine of "The Horse Dealer's Daughter," who, having succeeded in getting the doctor to surrender entirely to her, withdraws in fear from her victory. Will Brangwen determines to marry Anna and, afraid that she will leave him, becomes "abstract, purely a fixed will," feeling that if he relaxes his will, "he must be destroyed." And during this courtship, Will's defeat is foreshadowed. Like Siegmund of *The Trespasser,* he is "consumed, till he existed only as an unconscious, dark transit of flame, deriving from her."

In the third generation, the relationship of Ursula and Anton Skrebensky follows a similar to-and-fro but is even less sympathetic. Anton, who is less Victorian than Tom or Will, is not given to worship of the female; yet, like Tom and Will, he wants the woman to complete him. Early in his contact with Ursula we learn that Anton wished to "throw his detested carcase at her feet," and later Lawrence tells us of Anton's "mad dependence on her": "He felt himself a mere attribute of her." Only through Ursula can he come into being, escaping the nothingness and emptiness of himself, and so he confesses that "nothing else" but marriage means anything to him. Ursula is attracted to Anton as "one of the sons of God"; but as an independent modern woman, she is strongly inclined to assert her will over him. Their lovemaking becomes a game of provocation and challenge, "each playing with fire, not with love." Ursula "must ever prove her power," and Anton, kissing her, "asserts his will over her." So, Lawrence concludes: "It was a magnificent self-assertion on the part of both of them, he asserted himself before her, he felt himself infinitely male and infinitely irresistible, she asserted herself before him, she knew herself infinitely desirable, and hence infinitely strong. And after all, what could either of them get from such a passion but a sense of his or her own maximum self, in contradistinction to all the rest of life." So their plunge into African sensationalism is foreshadowed. The sympathetic impulses in both of them are weak, as if the change of civilization from the torpor of the Marsh to modern industrial society has caused an overdevelopment of the will at the expense of the sympathetic centers.

Marriage or Sexual Union versus Failure (The Battle of the Wills). After a period of conflict between voluntary and sympathetic desires, the male and the female, drawn irresistibly into connection, join in sexual union. When sexual union is perfect, the old self is given up; it dies in the tomb and womb of the unconscious, and one experiences a miraculous rebirth. A profound wonder and joy and a deep creative, purposive desire are awakened in the male. This point in the relationship between man and woman is crucial. If the man acts upon his desire to make a new world, he may move forward into the unknown, seeking to fight for a new society that promotes life and also reflects the wonder of his love. If, however, he fails to strive for a new heaven and a new earth, or if in sexual union he has not given up the self but remains intact, unchanged, a separate ego perversely using sex for ego consolation or ego aggrandizement, then the union or marriage breaks down, and a conflict of wills between man and woman is inevitable.

The first and perhaps the most important cause of the conflict is that the male, in seeking union with a woman, is really seeking a mother to give him unstinted love and to console him in his weakness. In short, the male is still a child, incapable of acting independently and not even aware of the Holy Ghost. In mating, such a male is motivated chiefly by his fear of being alone, unimportant, "nothing" in himself. Incapable of achieving "being," he tries to make the woman his raison d'être. But meaning and purpose can never be found in another creature, only in the infinite, in God, or in the ultimate connectedness of all things. The male's effort to make woman the be-all and end-all of existence satisfies neither him nor his woman. His deepest creative desires are frustrated, and because he puts the burden of life responsibility entirely upon the woman, she sees him as weak and childish, clinging to her as to a mother. Hence she rejects the man, and he, his ego insulted and betrayed ("I gave her my whole life, and she despises me"), retaliates in rage. The battle of wills commences. Carried to extremes it becomes reduction, or the desire to reduce the other person to inert matter. After the sympathetic connection between man and woman is broken, they become destructive. Hating the ego that defies them, they seek to destroy that antagonist. Lovemaking becomes ego assertion, or "conquest." The relationship of the lovers becomes that of the vampire to its victim or of the master to his slave. In its extreme forms, the lover becomes a sadist, a mad creature who, feeling himself to be helpless or impotent, seeks omnipotence—total control over another creature or over the whole of creation. Men would rather destroy the world than continue to live a meaningless life in which they feel "nullified."

Sometimes, if carried far enough, extremes of reduction may have a positive effect. Cruelty, perversity, sensationalism, or destruction may "unloose" or shatter the old self: corruption and death may breed new life; perversity may purge the soul. Having experienced the maximum of sensation, the soul may be ready for creative, not destructive, activity. On the other hand, extremes of reduction may issue, not in rebirth, but in death; the will to omnipotence may be carried to the point of absolute destruction of another person or of oneself. In each succeeding generation in *The Rainbow*, the couples move ever closer to the "passion of death," whose progress Lawrence traces so carefully in *Women in Love*.

In the first generation, as we have seen, Tom Brangwen, unable to develop as a purposive male, makes Lydia the be-all and end-all of his life.

In his dependence on her, he feels he is not strong enough to conquer and become the master; he fears that she is "not really his, it was not a real marriage, this marriage between them. She might go away." He cannot share her "foreign life," and he feels that for her he is only "a peasant, a serf, . . . a shadow, a nothing." His self-esteem wounded and his desire for fulfillment frustrated, he "stiffened with resistance." The battle of wills commences. From the extreme of self-obliteration, he recoils to the extreme of voluntary resistance. When, once again, Lydia turns to him, he "burst into flame for her, and lost himself." But so intense is his desire to possess her, to hold her sure and safe, so completely is his very being identified with her, that any sign of her indifference or self-sufficiency fills him with fear and rage. When she becomes pregnant, she is "not there for him"; he feels "deposed, cast out"; and his rage rises inevitably. Again and again the word *nothing* recurs as both male and female, seeking fulfillment from each other but unable to discover a meaning and purpose beyond themselves, feel the insignificance of their lives in the torpid Marsh. " 'To you I am nothing,' " Lydia says to Tom; " 'It is like cattle—or nothing.' " And he replies: " 'You make me feel as if *I* was nothing.' " It is not until Tom overcomes his "submission" to her and actively participates in sensual fulfillment that they experience a "transfiguration," and Tom travels "in her through the beyond."

The failure of a marriage unconnected with a higher purpose and goal is repeated in the second generation, but with a difference. For Will, Anna is the center of the great wheel of the universe. Ironically, she takes the place of the sun—the symbol of male creativity. She becomes "a more real day than the day could give." But his sexual fulfillment awakens all his purposive impulses. When Anna decides to give a tea party, this return to the old world that has become unreal to him frustrates his religious desire. Like Tom, he plunges into anger because he does not possess her and into "shame at his own dependence on her." She, on the other hand, resents his "futility" and his constant hovering about her in search of fulfillment.

For a time Will is compelled to "give everything to her, all his blood, his life, to the last dregs"; "there could be only acquiescence and submission." But his dependency and submission breed anger. Feeling her lack of respect for him, how she "jeered at his soul," he seeks to become "master-of-the-house," his will controlling hers. Each feels "nothing" to the other; each resents the other's self-sufficiency and separateness. Yet each fears being alone, and Will's dependency breeds shame, rage, and frustration. From his positive sympathy with Anna, he reacts into a "negative" voluntary resistance, provoking in turn her hatred of him. The lovers become separate wills fighting for triumph. Will, hating Anna's self-sufficiency, wishes to destroy her. He seeks to sever himself altogether from her, and he is "born for a second time" as a "separate identity, he existed alone." As a separate ego, he is driven into extremes of sensationalism and perversity, first seeking omnipotence in the triumph of his will (a "reducing force") over the girl from Nottingham, and then seeking with Anna a "passion of death," the perverse Absolute. "This supreme, immoral, Absolute Beauty, in the body of woman," in "pure darkness," this plunge into shame, carried to its final limits, liberates him. As noted [elsewhere], excess of activity in the mode of willful (or voluntary) sensuality awakens the desire for sympathetic activity in the spiritual mode. Will turns with interest to "public life," wants to "be unanimous with the whole of purposive mankind." As Lawrence summarizes, Will "had at length, from his profound sensual activity, developed a real purposive self." But Will does not have a vision of a greater society, and he ends up in "redbrick suburbia," serving the old dead world which he had wanted, after his marital bliss, to make new.

In the third generation the failure of love is repeated in the relationship of Ursula and Anton Skrebensky, but the failure is different from those in the first two generations. The relationship between Ursula and Anton is, almost from the beginning, a battle of wills. We have seen in the sheaves-gathering scene that Will and Anna vie for triumph. In an almost identical scene under the moon, Ursula becomes the "quarry and hound" together. Anton takes her into his arms "as if into the sure, subtle power of his will"; then, as they dance, "his will and her will" are "locked in a trance of motion." Like Helena in *The Trespasser,* Ursula, when the moon rises, offers herself to it for her "consummation," longing for "the coolness and entire liberty and brightness of the moon," while Anton's will strains "with all its tension to encompass [her] and compel her." But she is seized by a "sudden lust" to "tear him and make him into nothing." And she succeeds, destroying "the core" of him. Months later, when their lovemaking resumes, they plunge into African sensationalism, the jungle of willful sensuality. That denial of the spiritual and of the sympathetic centers leads toward death. Anton, knowing that "she did not esteem him" and feeling shame at his dependence on her, weeps like a child when Ursula tells him she does not want to marry him. Like the other half-developed males of this novel, he blurts that he cares for "nothing else" but marriage; but if Ursula's "fear of herself" tempts her to marry him, she is driven, once again, to destroy him when they again make love under the moon. This third generation, acting entirely from the voluntary will, achieves no sympathetic union and no rebirth.

The Search for Other Centers of Living: Work, Children, the Spiritual. All of the males in *The Rainbow* realize dimly that it is impossible to make woman into the Absolute and that there is something shameful in their dependency on woman; they need something greater, the veritable Absolute, not solely the darkness of unconsciousness in which the Spirit is denied. Thus Tom Brangwen, feeling that Lydia is "cold" and "selfish, only caring about herself," reflects: "He had to go out, to find company, to give himself away there. For he had no other outlet, he could not work to give himself out, he had not the knowledge." After the immersion in darkness, he is "elated" by the morning in which the male sun shines and the moon is "effaced on a blue sky." "Then he worked and was happy," Lawrence notes, "and the zest of life was strong in him." But Tom's physical work is meaningless to him; he feels himself "a prisoner . . . unadventurous" and wishes to "get out of this oppressive, shut-down, womanhaunt." The Marsh, that slough of the flesh, is "not enough." So casting about for the fulfillment he seeks, he turns to his daughter. He "formed another centre of love in her child, Anna"; and for a time the child, seeking her own Absolute, rejoices in his "big, unlimited being." But when Anna stiffens against him, he is filled with rage, and the relationship between father and child duplicates that between husband and wife. Tom's "joint activity" with Anna cannot possibly give him the support and solace he needs, and it is potentially dangerous to the child, who is not "set free" by her parents but for a time, like Hawthorne's Pearl, runs "hither and thither without relief."

Presently Tom's old desire to experience, if only vicariously, the life of the spirit prompts him to make Anna into "a lady," and when he visits his brother's mistress, he feels an "almost reverential admiration" for this woman who reads. Despising his own "poor way of life," he wants to "clamber out" of the "mud." But he cannot. His only fulfillment is to be found in his wife, mingling with her, "losing himself to find her, to find himself in her." He is able to overcome his Victorian inhibitions; and in joyous sensual fulfillment, man and wife enter "another circle of existence," discover "a new world." But the sensual fulfillment is not enough, and although Tom is proud of his marriage, he continues to yearn for "the further, the creative life" with Anna, "as if his hope had been in the girl." He has "nothing to show, no work" in his life—no creative work; and like most men, he can only hope that his children will do what he has failed to do in his own life.

In the next generation, Will Brangwen has a more highly developed sense of purpose than Tom. Will's carving of the phoenix suggests his strong urge towards rebirth and a new life; after his marriage with Anna, he is transformed: "So suddenly, everything that has been before was shed away and gone." So profoundly does love awaken his craving for the Absolute that now the world seems unreal: "peeled away into unreality, leaving here exposed the inside, the reality: One's own being, strange feelings and passions and yearnings and beliefs and aspirations, suddenly become present, revealed, the permanent bedrock, knitted one rock with the woman one loved." He feels that "the whole world could be divested of its garment, . . . and one could stand in a new world, a new earth, naked in a new, naked universe. It was too astounding and miraculous." For him at this point "the old outward order was finished. The new order was begun to last for ever, the living life, palpitating from the gleaming core, to action." But when he does not act upon this prompting to build a new heaven and a new earth, the marriage begins to break down. Then he turns, as Tom turned, to other centers of living.

The Church—which for him contains the All, in which are joined life and death, womb and tomb, light and darkness, spirit and flesh—gives Will his consummation. Yet Anna despises his mindless worship and destroys his passion for this dead symbol of the Absolute. The Cathedral becomes "dead matter" to him, though he still cherishes "the old, dear form of worship" and sometimes "lapses back [to the church] for his fulfillment." For a time, then, he remains passive, serving "the little matriarchy, nursing the child and helping with the housework, indifferent any more of his own dignity and importance." But he cannot long endure this "cabbage" existence, and still "passionate for something," he turns for fulfillment to his daughter, Ursula, as Tom had turned to Anna. Compulsively, Will seeks Ursula out "in a darkness" until they become "in the thick darkness, married." Ursula becomes the "light" to him, as Anna earlier had become the sun. His life is "based on her." When, inevitably, Ursula relapses "on her own violent will into her own separate world of herself," the connection between father and child is broken, and the battle of wills begins again, as it had in his marriage with Anna: "There was a curious fight between their two wills." Seeking the extreme of sensationalism, risking incest, Will begins to "dare" her to take violent risks with him. A "curious taunting intimacy" arises between them. When Ursula turns against him again, he searches for omnipotence through perversity. Then he is partially freed for purposive work.

In the third generation the search for other centers of living becomes most intense and adventurous. Ursula, after rejecting Christianity because she feels that the doctrine of love means the nullification of her pride and dignity, searches for one of "the sons of God." Skrebensky proves hollow. His only center of living, beyond her, is the nation state, which he serves blindly; he finds his Absolute in the blind collective will. In himself, he is "nothing," a man without a core. Ursula must seek elsewhere for religious purposiveness. She turns to Miss Inger, who argues plausibly that men "have lost the capacity for doing. . . . They make everything fit into an old, inert idea" and treat women as "an instrument" for this idea. But Miss Inger is a hideous creature of the will, one who worships "the impure abstraction, the mechanisms of matter." Then Ursula turns to "the man's world" of work and tries teaching, only to discover that here, too, "it was power, and power alone that mattered." Forced to bully others, she finds herself "subjugate to a bad, destructive will." And she recoils from the system, as she has earlier recoiled from herself with a "slow horror" when she has been seized by the desire to triumph over Skrebensky. Then she turns back, half in desperation, to Skrebensky and to a sensual darkness in which she is "shattered," "all dark, will-less, having only the receptive will." But this desperate plunge into mindless sensation, which represents a rejection of society and the light, is also a plunge towards death: once again, she is prompted to destroy Skrebensky with her "beaked harpy's kiss." Then, for a time, she is tempted to accept Skrebensky and her unborn child as "enough." Finally, after climbing free of the horses' threat—a symbolic climbing—and after seeing that she has been "trammelled and entangled" in a dead world, she imagines a rebirth, a breaking free from the shell like a kernel "thrusting forth the clear, powerful shoot." After a deep sleep, she begins to open like a flower to the new day; and the novel ends with her vision of a new world in which God is created in a social, political, and personal renaissance.

This brief summary of the laws of psychic interaction shows that Lawrence's "subjective science" was already highly developed in 1913 or 1914 when composition of *The Rainbow* began. If the novel is an allegory in the tradition of Bunyan or Spenser, it is even more impressively the culmination of nineteenth-century naturalism—of that effort to make literature scientific by explaining experience as exemplifying impersonal laws and by reducing human conduct to elemental motive forces or to material determinants.

How does Lawrence reconcile this scientific view of life with his religious view? How does he blend the voices of the angels of science and of religion? And how does he create, at the same time, a persuasive image of normal life? The angel of mimetic art has the difficult task of reconciling the claims of religion and of science while creating the illusion of reality and maximizing the emotional effects of the image of life.

THE ANGEL OF MIMETIC ART

Every character and every act must be seen from both the moral-allegorical and from the scientific point of view; yet the angel of mimetic art must avoid reducing characters either to mere allegorical counters or to simply electromagnetic forces. The characters must be real, their behavior convincingly normal. The mimetic artist must create an image of men and women like ourselves, whom we can care about. Three great problems must be solved: the problems of moral evaluation, of believability, and of sympathetic identification.

Consider first the problem of moral evaluation. The religious angel wishes to present characters in a moral framework, almost as allegorical counters, and to judge their conduct on the assumption that men, having free will, can choose the right path to the rainbow. The scientific angel wishes to present characters as impelled nilly-willy by dominant motive forces and by their temperamental make-up to act according to the strictest of laws. Can the artist have it both ways? — combine religion and scientific determinism? If Tom Brangwen is incapacitated from birth for the adventure into the unknown, how can he be condemned for failing to develop and grow? After all, Tom is very like an animal, destined from birth to illiteracy and life in the unconscious. We view him with the sort of sympathy, as well as detachment, that we might direct toward any suffering, bewildered, creature: because he is simply incapable of journeying toward the light, we pity his limitations and feel joy in his sensual fulfillment even as we might pity or take pleasure in the failures or triumphs of any honest animal. How then can he be condemned for his failures?

Lawrence's solution to this first problem is bold and simple. Tom Brangwen is not condemned; he condemns himself. "Oh, and he was shamed. He trampled himself to extinguish himself. . . . One was . . . never master of oneself." In *The Rainbow* the deep shame that all the males feel because of their utter dependency on women, because of their failure to develop, and because of their recurrent regressions into childish irresponsibility (as in the extraordinary scene in which Lydia is in labor and Tom longs for the "irresponsibility and security" of his boyhood) is a severe judgment on their lives.

In this way is Will Brangwen judged. Insofar as Will is blindly compelled to make first Anna and then Ursula the foundation of his being, he is not condemned: like Tom, he cannot help himself. Yet even though Will is driven by compulsion and is essentially "molelike," Lawrence suggests that Will, more highly developed than Tom, might have tried to face Anna's destructive criticism forthrightly. Will knows in his soul "what a fool he was, and was flayed by the knowledge"; he also knows that in seeking to arrogate his authority over Anna, "he had gone on the wrong tack." It is wrong, he knows dimly, to make woman the center of his existence; in some way, he knows, he exists in eternity, not just in time. He is conscious of his sin against the Holy Ghost but is unable to overcome his compulsions until, through "reduction," he is partially liberated.

In the third generation, however, a significant change occurs. Protestant individualism leads to the triumph of reason: every man is free to be a priest or a sinner. Free will enters the novel, as skepticism, already gaining force during the second generation in Anna, awakens all men to the knowledge that God is dead and all is permitted, though nothing, as Nietzsche would have added, is authorized. Ursula throws off blind religious faith and, condemned to existential freedom, confronts a world of like-minded individuals, men and women free to do anything they want to do. The question now becomes: how is this freedom to be used? For religious ends or for self-aggrandizement? For life or for death?

Skrebensky is condemned because, with knowledge and choice open to him, he remains a part of the undifferentiated mass, serving the state. Ursula condemns herself, recoiling in horror when she imposes her egoistic will on Skrebensky and destroys him. Miss Inger and Uncle Tom are condemned because they are conscious of good and evil: they see the alternatives but choose to follow the way of Moloch. And the educational system is condemned because educators allow bullying and materialism to supplant genuine life development. The point is not simply that awareness entails responsibility for one's acts. More than this, the condemned characters always condemn themselves, recognize that their choices violate their deepest, most holy promptings. Ursula's self-condemnation is the most obvious illustration; but even Uncle Tom, Miss Inger, and Skrebensky are aware of how deeply they violate life:

> Her Uncle Tom and her mistress remained there among the horde, cynically reviling the monstrous state and adhering to it, like a man who reviles his mistress, yet who is in love with her. She [Ursula] knew her Uncle Tom perceived what was going on. But she knew moreover that in spite of his criticism and condemnation, he still wanted the great machine. His only happy moments, his only moments of pure freedom were when he was serving the machines. Then, and then only, when the machine caught him up, was he free from the hatred of himself, could he act wholly, without cynicism and unreality.

> He too [Skrebensky] realised what England would be in a few hours' time—a blind, sordid, strenuous activity, all for nothing, fuming with dirty smoke and running trains and groping in the bowels of the earth, all for nothing. A ghastliness came over him.

> He was always active, cheerful, gay, charming, trivial. Only he dreaded the darkness and silence of his own bedroom, when the darkness should challenge him upon his own soul. That he could not bear, as he could not bear to think of Ursula. He had no soul, no background. He never thought of Ursula, not once, he gave her no sign. She was the darkness, the challenge, the horror. He turned to immediate things.

Self-condemned in the dark night of their souls, these characters obey the laws of psychic process even as they are subjected to a withering moral evaluation. Thus the scientific and the religious angels are admitted into the novel, and their antithetical demands are reconciled.

The problem of believability is more difficult to solve. The mimetic artist struggles to make the image of life persuasively real and authentic; but the angels of science and religion are bent on forcing the novel into surrealistic shapes. The angel of religion wants people who are two-dimensional moral abstractions, like the characters in Hawthorne's *The Marble Faun;* the angel of science wants to reduce people to voluntaristic and sympathetic oscillations, to compulsion neuroses, to automatism. The problem for the angel of mimetic art is to rescue life from doctrine, to preserve the complex whole of personality, and to present the subtle reality of organic life, against the reductions of science and the moral simplifications of religion. The people must be individuals, not just symbols or universal forces. A very special effort must be made to establish the characters as normal human beings immersed in daily living.

Here Lawrence's ability to capture the richness of normal domestic life, to see his people always in the context of unvaryingly ordinary domesticity, is indispensable. Tom Brangwen may be the Unconscious, the Flesh, the Blood; the to-and-fro of his actions may be an oscillation of voluntary and sympathetic forces; but unlike Hawthorne's Hilda or Donatello, Tom has a rich life beyond allegory, beyond intellectual abstraction. He is a farmer who likes to drink with his friends at the (symbolic) Red Lion; his speech is unvaryingly commonplace, tinged with "country" ironies; his habits are as predictable as those of the sun to which he turns his face. He is solidly there as a farmer, as a part of the Marsh, as husband, and as father.

Again, Will Brangwen may have been conceived of as a creature of the molelike darkness, blindly seeking fulfillment in the cathedral; but Will has a garden, and he gets angry when Ursula tramples it; he has his wife's tea party to contend with; he has his little fling in Nottingham. Embedded firmly in the particulars of daily life—a life so ordinary that "Pass the butter" and "It's a lovely day" are characteristic speeches—Will is never dissolved in allegorical or psychological abstractions. Should any of his behavior seem abnormal, Lawrence is always quick to shift from the frenzies of Will's unconscious mind to an objective perspective that restores our sense of his normality. Thus, after the terrible "Anna Victrix" chapter, in which Will suffers unspeakable pain and humiliation, we see him as part of the gathering at Baron Skrebensky's and learn that "Will Brangwen, ruddy, bright, with long limbs and a small head, like some uncouth bird, was not changed in the least." The passage underscores what is, I believe, a recurring experience in reading Lawrence: to realize with a shock that what Lawrence is always presenting, in language that captures the depth of unconscious experience, is life so commonnplace that it would be dismisssed by most writers as banal and undramatic: a young girl's first kiss or her infatuation with her boyfriend; a young couple's first discovery of the wonder of sex; a married couple's early misgivings—all so ordinary, yet so extraordinary, that Lawrence's fiction is truly, as Dr. Johnson might have said, a representation of "those passions and principles by which all minds are agitated." In *The Rainbow* there is nothing but normal sexual experience, normal living. This selection of materials from the most commonplace experiences of human beings is in large part what prevents the novel from becoming pure science or pure allegory.

Yet the handling of probabilities is never easy in this novel. The angel of science wants the characters to behave always according to the laws of psychic interaction. The battle of wills must always move toward reduction. Anna and Will *must* die of their perverse passion of death; and Will *must* be reborn, freed for work in the external world. Ursula *must* destroy Skrebensky, and later their following of the African way of pure mindless sensualism *must* issue in death of the soul. The mimetic artist must obviously take the greatest pains to make these extreme conclusions plausible. Does Lawrence succeed?

Most readers of *The Rainbow* do feel, from time to time, a certain forcing of the plot. Would Ursula really destroy Skrebensky with her "hard and fierce" kiss in the chapter entitled "First Love"? Is his annihilation inevitable? If we look carefully at the scene in which Anton is destroyed, we can see that Lawrence has provided entirely adequate causes for Anton's psychic death. In an earlier scene, in which Anton states that he will do whatever the state tells him to do, Ursula has told him bluntly that he isn't really "there," he is "nothing," a man without a core of belief, only a sodden acquiescence to the collective will. Thus, like Anna, she has undermined the only faith that her man has: she has already partially destroyed him. In addition, her virginal sense of her own power and of "the richness of her own life" prompts her to show him what a pitiful thing he is, to turn the tables on the male hunter: "A sudden lust seized her, to lay hold of him and tear him and make him into nothing." Finally, her youthful inability to understand the urgency of his sexual need, her indifference to his insistent physical demands, after she has roused him with her kiss, can only be interpreted as a devastating rebuff to his manhood, a kind of annihilation that many a young man has felt in such a situation. Anton has staked his entire manhood on his triumph over Ursula, but there wasn't any manhood there to stake!

The scene strikes me as plausible, then, even though it does not exhibit the sort of overwhelming inevitability that one sees in Will's attempts to "reduce" both the girl from Nottingham and Anna. Will always remains real to the reader, with the allegorical and scientific elements in his make-up dissolved into the persuasively rendered process of his development within normal surroundings. But Lawrence does not seem very interested in Skrebensky except as an allegorical figure — an army engineer who serves his country blindly and who fails to achieve "being." Skrebensky, more than any other character in *The Rainbow* (including Miss Inger or Uncle Tom), is a purely intellectual creation; and that he was willed onto the page is suggested by the fact that we know so little about his personal and domestic life. Lawrence had a clear idea of the man he wished to create; but the idea wasn't connected for Lawrence with the concrete particulars of life.

And yet — for there is always an "and yet" in discussing Lawrence — the psychology of Skrebensky's behavior is brilliant. The man who follows blindly the collective will of the nation, marching off to the Boer War mechanically, lacking belief in his "personal connection," and "dead" to his "own intrinsic life," has nothing to fall back upon, once the war is over, but "his five senses. They were to be gratified." So his plunge into African sensuality — the way of death — is inevitable. Equally inevitable is his turning, in his weakness, to Ursula and to marriage as his sole salvation, his becoming "helpless, at her mercy," and his pathetic weeping. By the same token, Ursula's destruction of him for a second time, with her "beaked harpy's kiss," is thoroughly prepared for. He stands for all that she resists and loathes in her soul — the hopelessness, the inertia, the terrible acceptance of a meaningless way of life. When she meets him again after the war, she knows "vaguely, in the first minute, that they were enemies come together in a truce." The destructive frictional to-and-fro of their relationship can only lead to the climax of psychic death.

Lawrence's handling of the ending of the novel has been generally attacked. Is Ursula's vision of the rainbow really, as John Worthen argues, a vision "which grows out of the particular needs of the author" rather than out of the novel itself? Is it really, as Leavis claims, "wholly unprepared and unsupported, defying the preceding pages"? In truth, the vision of the rainbow—that is, of Wholeness, of the perfect joining of light and dark, male and female, spirit and flesh—has hovered over the novel from the beginning. It appears at the end of the first-generation section, when Tom and Lydia achieve sensual consummation and Anna is set free to play "between the pillar of fire and the pillar of cloud in confidence, having the assurance on her right hand and on her left. She was no longer called upon to uphold with her childish might the broken end of the arch. Her father and her mother now met to the span of the heavens." It appears again at the end of the second-generation section, just prior to the shift to Ursula's life, when Anna, her child now born (but her husband defeated, "nullified"), strains to look at "something beyond":

> Anna loved the child very much, oh, very much. Yet still she was not quite fulfilled. She had a light expectant feeling, as of a door half opened. . . . She was straining her eyes to something beyond. And from her Pisgah mount, which she had attained, what could she see? A faint, gleaming horizon, a long way off, and a rainbow like an archway, a shadow-door with faintly coloured coping above it. Must she be moving thither?

Finally the vision appears at the end of the third-generation episodes. Ursula, more highly developed than Anna, more spiritually determined to throw off "the old, hard barren form of bygone living," has much the same vision, but a vision clarified, richer, and more meaningful than Anna's because it seeks to embrace the entire social and political future. The vision, like the rainbow, is "arched in [men's] blood" and seeks always to "quiver in their spirit." The vision is eternal; and this novel, as John Worthen beautifully describes it, is "the timeless account of impulse and aspiration and fulfilment, always modified and always re-enacted by each succeeding generation." The vision arises appropriately at the point when Ursula's child has been aborted and she is ready to resume a new way of life. The sudden brutal assault of the horses—those symbols of an oppressive brute sensual power, "never bursting free"—is connected with her pregnancy and with the threat to her further development: she has moved towards death in her following of the "African" way of pure sensation with Skrebensky. Now she must begin again. She turns to her vision of "the beyond"—to that which can free man from the tyranny of blind sensuality. She turns to the vision of Wholeness, and the eternal quest goes on.

It is apparent that Lawrence was in full control of his novel, including its conclusion. His control is particularly evident in his careful dramatization of the sufferings and joys of the characters while, at the same time, he stands aloof from them, regarding them with moral and scientific detachment in their struggles to achieve fulfillment and in their repeated failures. The distance had to be maintained; otherwise the scientific and religious character of the novel might be compromised; we might fail to see human experience with the proper ethical or scientific objectivity. But sympathetic identification with the characters is also necessary, for Lawrence wants us to feel the miracle of being alive and to understand life as it is lived, body and spirit fusing organically in the living moment. Hence Lawrence seeks, whenever possible, to see and experience everything from the point of view of each character, to imitate as accurately as possible each character's whole experience, conscious and unconscious, as the problem of finding fulfillment presents itself at successive stages of life. In short, Lawrence is determined to make his novel as dramatic as possible.

Lawrence would I think have liked Henry James's admonition "Dramatise! Dramatise!" as long as the "scenic method" did not blur our understanding of moral problems. Lawrence's novel is so thoroughly dramatized that even the passages which foreshorten, summarizing a character's experience and state of mind over several weeks or months (passages necessary and frequent in this three-generation novel), acquire the quality of felt life, partly because of the repetitive style, which imitates the pressure of a persistent desire, and partly because of the use of the Jamesian central consciousness (with the author looking over the character's shoulder and supplying information the character cannot supply). But Lawrence recognized that in order to harmonize the voices of the angels of science, religion, and mimetic art, point of view had to be flexible. To confine himself exclusively to the characters' points of view would be to present raw experience and raw feeling without understanding or evaluation. His problem then becomes that of simultaneously identifying with and critically appraising his people.

He has to have remarkable "negative capability": he has to treat his protagonists' experience with the utmost sympathetic imagination and with the utmost respect, assuming that the frightened, desiring, bewildered animal is always innocent in the sense that his deep desires and fears are not subject to conscious control. Then, drawing back, Lawrence has to register the full moral significance of each act. Thus when Lawrence wishes to judge harshly, he has to abandon the character's point of view. Neither Miss Inger nor Uncle Tom, for example, can be seen from within; both must be seen almost entirely from Ursula's point of view; the absence of sympathetic identification makes possible the severity of the judgment. But Lawrence is generally reluctant to present people entirely from another's point of view. His usual procedure is to identify wholly with a character for a time, dramatizing the character's immediate experience, and then quickly to shift the point of view to another character or to the narrator so as to register the moral significance of the action. The following passage is typical:

> It was so unutterably still and perfect with promise, the golden-lighted, distinct land, that Ursula's soul rocked and wept. Suddenly he glanced at her. The tears were running over her cheeks, her mouth was working strangely.
> "What is the matter?" he said.
> After a moment's struggle with her voice,
> "It is so beautiful," she said, looking at the glowing beautiful land. It was so beautiful, so perfect, and so unsullied.
> He too realised what England would be in a few hours' time—a blind, sordid, strenuous activity, all for nothing, fuming with dirty smoke and running trains and groping in the bowels of the earth, all for nothing. A ghastliness came over him.
> He looked at Ursula. Her face was wet with tears, very bright, like a transfiguration in the refulgent light. Nor was his the hand to wipe away the burning, bright tears. He stood apart, overcome by a cruel ineffectuality.
> Gradually a great, helpless sorrow was rising in him. But as yet he was fighting it away, he was struggling for his own life. He became very quiet and unaware of the things about him, awaiting, as it were, her judgment on him.
> They returned to Nottingham, the time of her examination came. She must go to London. But she would not stay with him in an hotel. She would go to a quiet little pension near the British Museum.
> Those quiet residential squares of London made a great impression on her mind. They were very complete. Her mind seemed imprisoned in their quietness. Who was going to liberate her?

Here Lawrence presents first Ursula's then Skrebensky's response to the beauty of the undefiled land. Ursula weeps for the hideous violation of the promise connected with the rainbow: a response commensurate with her passionate idealism, her search for one of the Sons of God. Skrebensky too is appalled in his soul as he considers the ghastly and pointless mutilation of beauty; but here the point of view shifts imperceptibly to that of the narrator, who delicately suggests both Skrebensky's incapacity for a deep sympathy and his moral inertia: "Nor was his the hand to wipe away the burning, bright tears.

He stood apart, overcome by a cruel ineffectuality." Having registered his moral disapproval, Lawrence returns immediately, however, to Skrebensky's point of view, defining with sympathy the man's struggle "for his own life," yet again suggesting Skrebensky's failure to assume responsibility and his weak submission to the female's judgment.

Foreshortening, moving with the utmost rapidity, Lawrence next resumes the objective narrative — "They returned to Nottingham" — and immediately shifts to Ursula's anticipation of her examination in London. Almost without transition, following the motions of her mind rather than her physical journeying, Lawrence places Ursula in London and, again employing her point of view, presents not only a sympathetic dramatization of her central problem ("Who was going to liberate her?") but also, very delicately, a moral evaluation of the society in which men and women submit passively, in "quietness," to the dead form of life.

Thus on half a page Lawrence shifts from Ursula to Anton to the narrator to Anton to the narrator and Ursula. Everywhere Lawrence conveys the immediacy of felt life even as he continues to exhibit the laws of life (the continuing frictional to-and-fro of Ursula and Skrebensky); and everywhere he interjects the delicate moral discriminations reflecting his thoughtful analysis of basic psychological, ethical, and social problems.

Thus the voices of the three angels are blended, and the image of life is charged with dramatic tension. Everywhere our concern for the characters, our fear that they will fail to "come through," is maximized. Everywhere Lawrence multiplies the difficulties of achieving connection and of building a rainbow. His understanding of the extent and the danger of the forces that prevent us from achieving wholeness of self and a healthy relationship between the self and the world is so comprehensive that almost anything in experience may be used to dramatize the soul's dilemma. Difficulties from within (the duality within the psyche) are compounded by those from without (the mechanistic industrial system that violates organic life; the educational system; the dead forms of social intercourse; the dead habits). And everywhere Lawrence intensifies our concern and dread by multiplying ironic reversals. Seeking salvation, the lover weds himself to a betrayer. Or a parent becomes a lover of his child, and all the horrors of incest are suggested. Again and again the loved one, the center of one's life, becomes a harpy, a vulture, a vampire. Again and again people are driven toward compulsive cruelty and insane aggression. Again and again Lawrence provides vivid renderings of the anguish and frenzy of the soul as it is thwarted and driven blindly to find a frightening fulfillment or compensation. Fear and horror are intensified as we witness innocent creatures driven to extremes of perversity; and the horror is the greater because it is contrasted with stirring depictions of ecstasy and fulfillment. So precious is the goal, so powerful is the need for fulfillment, that any rupture of the connection, any break in the arch, acquires a singular dreadfulness. A slight jeering intonation stirs madness in the soul. The unique power of the "Anna Victrix" chapter — surely the best thing that Lawrence ever wrote! — derives largely from the terrifying momentum, the frightening compounding, of destructiveness. After the Edenic bliss in the marriage bed, the bed becomes a hearse; the bride becomes a demon; the groom is driven into a frenzy of retaliation. There is Gothic melodrama in this, but the dread and horror that arise from the inversion of all expectation and from the perversion of all innocent desire are the dread and horror of normal psychic experience. The laws of psychic interaction become the laws of ironic reversal, and Lawrence's analysis of the psyche becomes magnificent art.

Most remarkable is, as F. R. Leavis has suggested, Lawrence's ability to record with full intensity the actual experience of life and simultaneously to stand back as an impersonal observer, evaluating, analyzing causal relationships, and defining meanings with the utmost precison. There was always in Lawrence's work the danger that the allegorizing would get the upper hand and drive life from the novel, as when Lawrence invited Ciccio into *The Lost Girl* or Cipriano into *The Plumed Serpent.* In *The Rainbow* the three strange angels all sing out with strong voices in a miraculous harmony.

We need a name to suggest the uniqueness of the form Lawrence created. Recognizing that the book presents, from the perspective of "the vast, unexplored morality of life itself," the story of Western man's quest for fulfillment of all his deepest desires, we would approach adequate definition, I think, if we called the novel a psychological epic-romance, or perhaps a psychological mimetic allegory. The method is "exhaustive" because the book supplies the natural, cultural, and psychological framework within which the experience of every man and woman may be evaluated with a recognition of its moral significance in the timeless quest for balance and the fulfillment of man's deepest desires. If every effort must be made to maximize sympathy for the protagonists, one must never be allowed to identify with them completely: they must always be seen sharply as the fallible, passion-ridden creatures they are. The action must lay bare the causes of their suffering and their partial fulfillments and of their immorality and their goodness, from the point of view of "the vast, unexplored morality of life itself." The excellence of the novel arises largely from Lawrence's discovery of the mean between the particularization of experience in the interest of mimetic fidelity and the abstraction from experience of essential psychological patterns and of the moral principles inherent in each stage of the human struggle to achieve maximum of being.

Chronology

1885	David Herbert Lawrence is born on September 11 in Eastwood, a Nottingham mining village, the fourth child of Arthur Lawrence, a coal miner, and Lydia Beardsall Lawrence, a former schoolteacher of lower-middle-class background.
1898–1901	Attends Nottingham High School on a County Council Scholarship.
1901	Meets Jessie Chambers, who becomes his childhood amour and the model for "Mirriam Leivers" of *Sons and Lovers;* goes to work for a dealer in artificial limbs.
1902–6	Becomes pupil-teacher at British School at Eastwood; begins writing *The White Peacock* and poems. Engaged to Jessie Chambers.
1906–8	Attends Nottingham University College, taking the teacher's certificate course.
1908–11	Teaches at the Davidson Road Boy's School; Jessie Chambers sends some of his poems to Ford Madox Hueffer's *English Review,* where Lawrence's poetry is first published in the November 1909 issue. Friendship with Helen Corke, a schoolteacher.
1910	Starts writing *The Trespasser;* engagement with Jessie broken off; starts writing *Paul Morel* (to become *Sons and Lovers*). His mother dies of cancer, December 10.
1911	His first novel, *The White Peacock,* is published by Heinemann in January.
1912	Falls ill and gives up teaching. Introduced to Frieda von Richthofen Weekley, the thirty-two-year-old wife of his former French professor at University College, Nottingham. *The Trespasser* published in May. Lawrence and Frieda elope,

travelling together in Germany and Italy. Finishes *Sons and Lovers;* writes plays, stories and poems.

1913   *Sons and Lovers* published in May. *The Insurrection of Miss Houghton* (to become *The Lost Girl*) begun. Works on draft of *The Sisters* (to become *Women in Love* and *The Rainbow*); writes tales published as *The Prussian Officer* (1914). Meets John Middleton Murry.

1914   Frieda divorces Weekley and marries Lawrence. *Study of Thomas Hardy* written, and work continues on *The Sisters.*

1915   *The Rainbow* published in September, suppressed for "indecency" in November. Writes "The Crown."

1916   Lives in Cornwall, finishes writing *Women in Love.*

1917   Denied passport to U.S.; rejected as medically unfit for military service; expelled by military from Cornwall on suspicion of spying.

1918   Drafts *Movements in European Literature,* the play *Touch and Go,* and *The Fox.*

1919   Writes tales published as *England, My England;* drafts *Aaron's Rod;* returns to Continent: Florence, Capri, Taormina.

1920   *Women in Love* is privately printed in New York. Completes and publishes *The Lost Girl;* writes *Birds, Beasts and Flowers, Psychoanalysis and the Unconscious* (1921), and a novel, *Mr. Noon.*

1921   Writes *Fantasia of the Unconscious* (1922), *The Captain's Doll,* and *The Ladybird.*

1922   Visits Ceylon and Australia, where he writes most of *Kangaroo. Aaron's Rod* published in April. Takes up residence in Taos, New Mexico.

1923   Completes and publishes *Birds, Beasts and Flowers; Kangaroo* published; begins work on *The Plumed Serpent.* Visits Mexico and Europe.

1924   Writes *Mornings in Mexico* (1927), *St. Mawr* (1925), and the tales, *The Princess* and *The Woman Who Rode Away.*

1925   Completes *The Plumed Serpent* and the play *David. St. Mawr* published.

1926   *The Plumed Serpent* published in January. Takes up residence near Florence. Begins writing *Lady Chatterley's Lover.*

1927   Begins work on *Escaped Cock* (published as *The Man Who Died*) and *Etruscan Places* (1932).

1928   Completes *Lady Chatterley's Lover,* published first in Florence, though numerous pirated editions appear in England. Resides in South of France. Postal authorities seize manuscript of *Pansies.* Completes *The Man Who Died* (1929).

1929   Police raid exhibition (July) of Lawrence's paintings at the Warren Gallery, London. Writes *More Pansies, Pornography and Obscenity, Apocalypse,* and *Nettles.*

1930   Dies of tuberculosis at a sanatorium near Antibes, France, on March 2.

1960   Penguin Books publishes unexpurgated *Lady Chatterley's Lover* in England and is prosecuted under the Obscene Publications Act. After a celebrated trial, Penguin wins.

Contributors

HAROLD BLOOM, Sterling Professor of the Humanities at Yale University, is the author of *The Anxiety of Influence, Poetry and Repression*, and many other volumes of literary criticism. His forthcoming study, *Freud: Transference and Authority*, attempts a full-scale reading of all of Freud's major writings. A MacArthur Prize Fellow, he is general editor of five series of literary criticism published by Chelsea House. During 1987–88, he served as Charles Eliot Norton Professor of Poetry at Harvard University.

ALAN FRIEDMAN is Professor of English at the University of Illinois. He is the author of *The Turn of the Novel*, among other works.

COLIN CLARKE is the author of *Romantic Paradox: An Essay on the Poetry of Wordsworth* and *River of Dissolution: D. H. Lawrence and British Romanticism*.

SCOTT SANDERS is Professor of English at Indiana University and the author of *D. H. Lawrence: The World of the Five Major Novels*.

EVELYN J. HINZ is Professor of English at the University of Manitoba and the author of *The Mirror and the Garden: Realism and Reality in the Writings of Anaïs Nin*.

ROBERT KIELY is Professor of English at Harvard University and the author of *The Romantic Novel in England* and *Beyond Egotism*.

DANIEL J. SCHNEIDER is Professor of English at the University of Tennessee, Knoxville, and the author of *D. H. Lawrence: The Artist as Psychologist*.

Bibliography

Adam, Ian. "Lawrence's Anti-Symbol: The Ending of *The Rainbow*." *The Journal of Narrative Technique* 3 (May 1973): 77–84.

Adamowski, T. H. "*The Rainbow* and 'Otherness.'" *D. H. Lawrence Review* 7 (Spring 1974): 311–34.

Alinei, Tamara. "Imagery and Meaning in DHL's *The Rainbow*." *Yearbook of English Studies* 2 (1972): 205–11.

Alldritt, Keith. *The Visual Imagination of D. H. Lawrence*. Evanston, Ill.: Northwestern University Press, 1971.

Balbert, Peter. *D. H. Lawrence and the Psychology of Rhythm: The Meaning of Form in* The Rainbow. The Hague: Mouton, 1974.

Berthout, Jacques. "*The Rainbow* as Experimental Novel." In *D. H. Lawrence: A Critical Study of the Major Novels and Other Writings,* edited by A. H. Gomme. New York: Harper & Row, 1978.

Blanchard, Lydia. "Mothers and Daughters in D. H. Lawrence: *The Rainbow* and Selected Shorter Works." In *Lawrence and Women,* edited by Ann Smith. London: Vision, 1978.

Brandabur, A. M. "The Ritual Corn-Harvest Scene in *The Rainbow*." *D. H. Lawrence Review* 6 (Fall 1973): 284–302.

Burns, Robert. "The Novel as Metaphysical Statement: Lawrence's *The Rainbow*." *Southern Review* (Australia) 4 (1973): 139–60.

Chrisman, Reva Wells. "Ursula Brangwen and the University: D. H. Lawrence's Rejection of Authority in *The Rainbow*." *Kentucky Philological Association Bulletin* (1974): 9–16.

Clarke, Colin. *River of Dissolution: D. H. Lawrence and English Romanticism.* New York: Barnes & Noble, 1969.

Draper, R. P. "*The Rainbow*." *Critical Quarterly* 20 (Autumn 1978): 49–64.

Eagleton, Terry. *Exiles and Emigres: Studies in Modern Literature.* New York: Schocken, 1970.

Effron, Arthur. "Toward a Dialectic of Sensuality and Work." *Paunch* 44–45 (May 1976): 152–70.

Gamache, Lawrence B. "The Making of an Ugly Technocrat: Character and Structure in Lawrence's *The Rainbow*." *Mosaic* 12, no. 1 (1978): 61–78.

Goldberg, S. L. "*The Rainbow:* Fiddle-Bow and Sand." *Essays in Criticism* 11 (1961): 418–34.

Goodheart, Eugene. *The Utopian Vision of D. H. Lawrence.* Chicago: The University of Chicago Press, 1985.

Heldt, Lucia Henning. "Lawrence on Love: The Courtship and Marriage of Tom Brangwen and Lydia Lensky." *D. H. Lawrence Review* 8 (Fall 1975): 358–70.

Hill, Ordelle G., and Potter Woodbery. "Ursula Brangwen of *The Rainbow:* Christian Saint or Pagan Goddess?" *D. H. Lawrence Review* 4 (Fall 1971): 274–79.

Hinz, Evelyn J. "*The Rainbow:* Ursula's 'Liberation.'" *Contemporary Literature* 17 (Winter 1976): 24–43.

Holderness, Graham. *D. H. Lawrence: History, Ideology and Fiction.* Dublin: Gill & McMillan, 1982.

Howe, Marguerite Beede. *The Art of the Self in D. H. Lawrence.* Athens: Ohio University Press, 1977.

Hughes, Richard. "The Brangwen Inheritance: The Archetype in D. H. Lawrence's *The Rainbow.*" *Greyfriar* 17 (1976): 33–40.

Kay, Wallace G. "Lawrence and *The Rainbow:* Apollo and Dionysus in Conflict." The *Southern Quarterly* 10, no. 3 (April 1972): 209–22.

Kennedy, Andrew. "After Not So Strange Gods in *The Rainbow.*" *English Studies* 63 (June 1982): 220–30.

Kermode, Frank. *D. H. Lawrence.* New York: Viking, 1973.

Kondo, Kyoko. "The Rainbow in Focus: A Study of the Form of *The Rainbow* by D. H. Lawrence." *Studies in English Literature* (Tokyo) (1985): 53–69.

Leavis, F. R. *Thought, Words and Creativity: Art and Thought in D. H. Lawrence.* New York: Oxford University Press, 1976.

McLaughlin, Ann L. "The Clenched and Knotted Horses in *The Rainbow.*" *D. H. Lawrence Review* 13 (Summer 1980): 179–86.

Meyers, Jeffrey. "*The Rainbow* and Fra Angelico." *D. H. Lawrence Review* 7 (Summer 1974): 139–56.

Mueller, W. R. "D. H. Lawrence: The Paradisal Quest." In *Celebration of Life,* 144–68. New York: Sheed & Ward, 1972.

Nixon, Cornelia. "To Procreate Oneself: Ursula's Horses in *The Rainbow.*" *ELH* 49, no. 1 (Spring 1982): 123–42.

Raddatz, Volher. "Lyrical Elements in D. H. Lawrence's *The Rainbow.*" *Revue des Langues Vivantes* 40, no. 3 (1974): 235–42.

Raina, M. L. "The Wheel and the Centre: An Approach to *The Rainbow.*" *Literary Criterion* (India) 9 (Summer 1970): 41–55.

Ross, Charles L. "The Revisions of the Second Generation in *The Rainbow.*" *Review of English Studies* 27 (August 1976): 277–95.

Scheckner, Peter. *Class, Politics, and the Individual: A Study of the Major Works of D. H. Lawrence.* Cranbury, N.J.: Fairleigh Dickinson University Press, 1985.

Schleifer, Ronald. "Lawrence's Rhetoric of Vision: The Ending of *The Rainbow.*" *D. H. Lawrence Review* 13 (Summer 1980): 161–78.

Schwartz, Daniel R. "Lawrence's Quest in *The Rainbow.*" *Ariel* 11, no. 3 (1980): 43–66.

Smith, Frank. *D. H. Lawrence: The Rainbow.* Studies in English Literature, no. 46. London: E. Arnold, 1971.

Squires, Michael. "Recurrence as Narrative Technique in *The Rainbow.*" *Modern Fiction Studies* 21 (Summer 1975): 230–36.

Stoll, John E. *The Novels of D. H. Lawrence: A Search for Integration.* Columbia: University of Missouri Press, 1971.
Worthen, John. *D. H. Lawrence and the Idea of the Novel.* London: Macmillan, 1979.

Acknowledgments

"*The Rainbow*: A 'Developing Rejection of Old Forms' " (originally entitled "A 'Developing Rejection of Forms' ") by Alan Friedman from *The Turn of the Novel* by Alan Friedman, © 1966 by Alan Friedman. Reprinted by permission.

"Reductive Energy in *The Rainbow*" by Colin Clarke from *River of Dissolution: D. H. Lawrence and English Romanticism* by Colin Clarke, © 1969 by Colin Clarke. Reprinted by permission of Barnes & Noble Books, Totowa, New Jersey, and Routledge & Kegan Paul Ltd.

"Nature vs. Society in *The Rainbow*" by Scott Sanders from *D. H. Lawrence: The World of the Five Major Novels* by Scott Sanders, © 1973 by Scott Sanders. Reprinted by permission.

"The Paradoxical Fall: Eternal Recurrence in *The Rainbow*" (originally entitled "The Paradoxical Fall: Eternal Recurrence in D. H. Lawrence's *The Rainbow*") by Evelyn J. Hinz from *English Studies in Canada* 3, no. 4 (Winter 1977), © 1977 by the Association of Canadian University Teachers of English. Reprinted by permission of the Association.

"A Long Event of Perpetual Change: *The Rainbow*" (originally entitled "A Long Event of Perpetual Change: Marriage") by Robert Kiely from *Beyond Egotism* by Robert Kiely, © 1980 by the President and Fellows of Harvard College. Reprinted by permission of Harvard University Press.

"The three Angels in *The Rainbow*" by Daniel J. Schneider from *D. H. Lawrence: The Artist as Psychologist* by Daniel J. Schneider, © 1984 by the University Press of Kansas. Reprinted by permission.

Index